The Story of an
EDUCATION

The Story of an
EDUCATION

SHAMBO DEY

PARTRIDGE
A Penguin Random House Company

To order additional copies of this book, contact
Partridge India
000 800 10062 62
orders.india@partridgepublishing.com

www.partridgepublishing.com/india

To Aditya, for your support

All differences in this world are of degree, and not of kind, because oneness is the secret of everything.

…Swami Vivekananda

PROLOGUE

It was 11 o'clock on an autumn morning. I was leaping through the college lobby, hoping to make it to the lecture hall. The first class of the day was Network Security. Near the notice board, a large crowd had gathered. The guys were throwing themselves upon each other to get a look at the notices pasted there. I had neither a minute to spare nor the energy to navigate my way to the front of the crowd. I would see the notice later on, I decided.

I found a seat my two best friends had held for me in the last row of the hall. For three long years, we have been sitting there. By now, our names had been etched into the bare bones of these seats, literally and metaphorically. Already, the professor had switched on the projector and started to draw one of his favourite mesh diagrams on a white board on the other side. I settled down inside a class of engineers humming very softly.

"The placements are going to begin in less than four weeks." I heard a low tensed voice mumble behind me. "The notice has come up. Did you see it?"

"Yes, I have and I can't think of anything else right now," replied another, "The time for us has come."

"Last year, Infosys hired only sixty five guys and the rest went to TCS and Wipro. This time they are betting that IBM might be coming to the campus. If that is really true, then I should better start preparing for their interviews. I have already forgotten most of what we have learned so far."

"What would the annual package be like this time?"

"I don't know. Last year, the packages were lower. But let's hope that this time it will go past three lacs."

"Hey, what do you want to do with your first pay?"

"The first thing I want is an iPhone."

Trying to ward off their thoughts, I aimed my focus on the lecture for a while.

Another conversation wheezed into my ears, this time from the row in front of me.

"How did your CAT exam go?"

"I am really worried that I might miss the 99th percentile unless I get enough correct answers in the quant section. If I don't get through this year, I am planning to lock myself up and prepare harder for next year."

"My quant section was fine but I messed up in the verbal. But you know, I met a guy at our coaching class, who had got 99.5 and 99.2 in two consecutive years and he was still rejected by the IIMs."

"I think he did not do enough mock interviews before showing up at A, B, C."

I sat in the middle of this, wondering. On any other day, we would have, by now, dozed off with fish eyes. But not today. There was an unknown anxiety and fervour in the room, not the usual boredom. I felt the pulse and glanced at my two friends. A look meant more than a thousand words: *what are you thinking?*

Well, I was not really thinking of a way to bunk the next class. I was pondering on something else, the time before I became an engineer. I hailed from a family that ran a small but profitable business. They made enough to put me in one of the premier Missionary schools in the country. At school, my mind had opened in manifold directions, particularly in fine arts and sports. I was strong enough in academics to get cross the 95 percent line, earning the luxury to pursue whatever field of study I wanted to.

Although my real interest was in literature, I did not really have my way. My father said, "You can read all your literature later on. You have your whole life for that. I want you to become someone first. I want you to do what all your friends are going to do- become an engineer." Over the two years that followed, I had blindly followed the ranks of almost all my classmates and burned the oil of our midnight lamps to fulfil what was the common wish of all our parents.

In those two years, I had no choice but to try very hard to understand mathematics and natural sciences but these courses simply had too many brute facts to memorize. Yet once in college, I planned to spend my years living as authentically and ecstatically as possible. I managed to find a few smart and quirky people: people like myself. I didn't have any academic pretensions and didn't work very hard at my studies, and with the stiff competition I got mediocre grades– I think my overall college average was something between B and C. Instead of studying, I was walking around the grassy campus, talking to new friends, reading newly-released books, relishing the taste of alcohol for the first time and enjoying the chance to be around girls, freed from the shackles of an all-male school.

But now in last lap of college, I had suddenly begun to feel queasy about my future. In a short while from now, I might be working for one of the three titans of India's technology world, Infosys, Wipro or TCS in one of their shinning technology parks. I took a deep breath staring down the abyss of my reality.

All this was playing like a tape at the back of my mind as I stared at the white board in the classroom which was already full of illegible diagrams of routers, gateways and backbone LANs. I summoned all my mental energies to concentrate for a few seconds but my mind wavered again like a flickering candle in the winnowing wind. Was I going to do anything different at all? I would mint money, like many of my friends. Perhaps twice or thrice the average Indian. But I looked at the mirror and I was nowhere to be found, caught in the swamp of the hopes of my father, my mother, my brother, my teachers and my friends. I had chosen this stream and perhaps also this career because it was labelled as the only worthwhile thing to do. I had never asked myself any questions. Did it really matter to me? Or, is there anything else I am capable of doing?

More thoughts spilled over. The lectures that day seemed to puncture my spirits. For the first time in four years, I disliked being inside this envelope of complacency. I thought harder still, until my head was totally fogged with confusion. In the end I concluded that this was only a passing phase and time will take care of things.

Two and a half nights later, I received quite an unexpected call from an old school friend and another engineering graduate like me. He was calling from his hostel room.

"Hey, are you awake?"

I was.

"I wanted to tell you about a great presentation we had on our campus today." There was a tinge of genuine excitement in his tone. "It was delivered by a new and very young organisation set up in Bombay. It's called Teach For India. They are out recruiting some of the brightest college graduates for a life-changing experience of teaching in the slums of Bombay and Pune. It is agonizingly tough to get in. Plus, you have to commit two years of your life, trying to change the education and future of the poorest children in India. When the talk was on, the only person I could think of fit for this kind of life was you."

Although my friend was unaware of it, I had some experience of tutoring a boy who lived close to my house for a year and a half and made some pocket money in the process. But he wasn't one of those children who slug against car windows, run around the aisles of traffic with naked feet or sing songs on local trains for money.

I replied, "No thanks. I will pass."

He tried to argue for a while but seeing that I was not obliging he did not press any further. But as he hung up, he said, "Remember, this is not for those who are ordinary."

I trusted my friend's words though and visited the website, eventually. The application process to get selected at Teach For India was a long one. One would have to fill in an application, full of essays, which would be followed by an in-person assessment and a final stage interview, the entire process taking more than three months to complete.

A few days later, three of us had bunked college and we were sitting at a safer place by the side of a quiet lake, a few kilometres away from the din and buzz of the city.

"I want to do something much more than writing codes, something outside this box." I told them about Teach For India.

One of my friends broke into laughter almost instantly. "Are you going to be a teacher? That's really funny! You don't even look like one. What are you going to teach children- A for apple, B for ball and C for cat?" We all laughed for a while, as we remembered the jokes we had about some of our own school teachers.

"I think it takes one a lot of courage to do this kind of work," said my other friend finally.

A few minutes of silence passed between the three of us.

"Only one day is left for the application deadline," I remembered. "Fuck."

Little did I feel that the winter of my life, the harbinger of warmth, was about to be over when in early December I received a call from an unknown number.

"Hello, we are calling from Teach For India. We are pleased to invite you to the next round of our application process."

I was elated. Several thousands had already fallen by the wayside; among the vanquished were many champions of Harvard, Yale and the IITs. Now, it was the best against the best.

"In the second round," she continued, "you are required to present a lesson to a panel of interviewers. You will get only 5 minutes of time to do this. This would be followed by a group discussion and problem solving round and then you might receive an invitation to a final one-on-one interview."

I was almost at my wit's end. If until now, I was feeling like Christ cruising through Jerusalem, I was now the Prophet on the cross. Five minutes was only a pinch of time. What could I possibly teach in that time? I had no idea.

Over the next few days, I went through several primary and middle school text books until I found a piece that had caught my own interest as a student. I prepared a small write up from a couple of books. But teaching a class for just five minutes seemed harder than said. I tried to put all the knowledge I had acquired in my life but it was of no help. I went over my lesson at least fifteen times and every time I lacked the poise and the clarity of a teacher's voice. I practiced time and time again before the mirror, trying very hard to put on the façade of my middle school history teacher. She was a calm and controlled old lady and yet she carried an authority that no one could match. This contrast was extremely difficult to adopt. How did she do it so naturally? I modulated my voice in umpteen ways, hoping to get as close to her as I could. It seemed as if I was preparing dialogues for a theatre show.

Finally it was showtime. Perspiring like a cornered rat, I somehow taught my lesson to the other participants and two hawkish Americans. The tension was visible to the interviewer as well and I worried that my lesson and subsequent interview had not gone the way I would have liked it to. I was filled with a fear that I had made some minor mistake, or worse, said something awful that I didn't realize. Did I appear more like a geek and less like a teacher? Was I too boring and unenergetic to them? While I felt I gave my interviewers a full and vibrant picture of who I am, what if who I am is not what they are looking for? In other words I tried to imagine every possible thing that made me feel more miserable afterwards than on the day of the interview.

In the same month, our college placements began for the year. The biggest brand names of India's thriving Silicon Valley came to our campus with promises and hopes of a better future. The economy was also in great shape- growing at 9% per annum and with a strong demand for software exports. It was like a festival all over the campus. Fourth year students had never been busier. Even the juniors were curious all the time, trying to get as much inside information from their seniors as they could. There was widespread speculation over what sort of questions could come for our aptitude tests and what books one needs to read for that. Some of us had called up our seniors to find out what they knew. Needless to say, the vast majority of us got selected for the final interviews.

Compared to Teach For India, the recruitment process at an IT company takes just about half an hour to complete. The whole pursuit of engineering was compressed into that single half hour slot spent with the interviewer, and by the time the next candidate's turn came, we had put a job in our pockets. The next day, most of us had bagged their second offers. And their third offers on the third day. I had secured two very promising offers. I had forgotten about Teach For India for a while because no reply had come until then. I forced myself to believe that I did not make it through. But then a phone call came one afternoon when I was on my way home from college.

"We are calling from Teach For India", said the same voice, "We would like to offer you a place in our next cohort."

I could hardly believe what she had just said. "Really, is it true? Are you sure? Can you please repeat it?"

"Yes, and you would be receiving your offer letter within three days."

I was overwhelmed and I could not think straight. Even before the caller hung up, I had begun to imagine myself standing before a class full of eager faces with a piece of chalk in my hand. I imagined teaching them every possible piece of fact or information I knew from science to literature, arts and sports.

But slowly an unpleasant feeling came down upon me like a thunderstorm on a summer day. A couple of weeks ago, I had brought home those coveted tech jobs, much like a trophy wife, that made my folks feel so proud of me that I was driven to my wit's end with their congratulatory calls. What am I going to tell them now? I knew what they would all say- did you study so hard all your life to become *this*? True, I was going to take a profession that society doesn't remotely consider as distinguished. I would not even be making half the money that my friends would make.

As expected, there was utter shock and confusion, followed only by glaring disappointment on everyone's faces.

"Why are you going to teach?" my father oppugned.

"What are you going to achieve out of this job?" my uncle questioned.

"What are going to do afterwards?" my mother asked.

"Do you even realize how it is going to hamper your long-term career?" our neighbour remarked.

It made no sense to them. I knew there wasn't really much that I could say to convince them and they knew there wasn't much they could do either to dispel my enthusiasm. I had made my decision.

ONE

My life has been spent entirely in East India, which had left large parts of the country relatively unknown in my eyes. In the days leading up to my departure, I had however tried my best to learn anything I could about Pune, the Queen of the Deccan.

Once a battleground for the territorial dominion of the subcontinent, the city was now one pullulating with high tech parks, world-class universities, international business centres and spacious malls- a thriving testament to a country's passage into modernity. My first month here was spent in a pot of paradise- a lush boot camp located on the top of a hill, thirty odd kilometres off the din of the bustling city. The camp could be easily mistaken by one to be a five-star resort cast against the wild, but in perfect harmony with it. Over the shoulders of the hill, the city looked like a cascade of Legos speckled with tiny yellow dots in the evening. But nothing that I had read or seen could give me a complete picture of the place and left me wanting to know only more about the place and the people who inhabited it. At the close of the summer, I received my appointment and started hunting for a flat. In a couple of days, with the aid of a few close friends, I found a flat in a neighbourhood located nearly in the heart of the city and began preparations for school. I had brought with me mostly books, journals and diaries and everything else that I had enjoyed reading as a child. I had not yet seen my students but I hoped firmly that their ballooning minds would enjoy all of the same things as I did.

The school that I was going to teach in could not be traced using Google. It was located in an enormous slum that in itself was within a vast underbelly of the city that was known as the Peth. About five kilometres in diameter, this part of Pune is a juxtaposition of long stretches of unending and densely populated slums, more than twenty five in numbers which are packaged in one box. My simple research had told me that historically, the Peths developed different characters: Kasba and Somwar were residential, Visapur was home to many military institutions, while Malkapur had a bazaar. In Murtazarad, well-to-do families built their homes close to the Peshwa of Pune, Sadashiv Peth became a center for Brahmin orthodoxy, while Budhwar Peth was primarily a business district. Although the Peths were cast-based localities, they were not totally segregated. In the end of the eighteenth century, seven of the old Peths were renamed after the days of the week by the powerful minister Nana Phadnis, who also had a Peth named after himself, Nana Peth, where my school was located.

It was the British that left the Peths to themselves and built their own residential areas, cantonments, planned communities on a grid pattern and while the rest of Pune flourished over the course of time, the Peths decayed into squatter settlements mostly filled with refugees. And, as

I later learned, having one of the worst literacy rates in the country. Now, like a liquid filling up a container, the spaces between these slums settlements was filled up by overcrowded wholesale markets, eateries, industrial units, schools and hospitals.

My school was not navigable by auto-rickshaws or buses but only bicycles. I did not have a bicycle, so my only recourse was to walk through the slums.

I had with me no address but only a rough mental assumption of the direction in which the school was situated. Early in that morning, I reached one of the avenues of the Peth by a public bus where I got off to cross the road and take a lane that went squarely towards the west. This area was called Bhawani Peth, named after the goddess Bhawani Mata. I walked a bit aimlessly through the street, looking here and there and trying to register the buildings and the landmarks in my mind. Within about two minutes of walking, the complexion of the roads changed. An unending necklace of old houses stood closely with their shoulders pressed against each other leaving so little space that even a fly could not be squeezed in. They were mostly slums that looked more like ant colonies built on a jumble of planks and daubs. There were numerous pan shops, ration shops and all kinds of small garages and factories dealing in iron, steel, wood and other wares. All along these narrow arteries, I encountered a veritable mosaic of races, religions, provinces and languages- Marathis, Tamils, Telegus, Biharis, Gujaratis and a disproportionate portion of the Muslims.

Besides the multitude of human swarms, I passed by herds of giant buffalos with red horns that tucked their mouths inside heaps of garbage, which were as tall as actual houses, and waged their tails to keep pestering mosquitos and flies away. Several crows and goats sprinkled around them, competing with one another to secure a share of this free breakfast. The air smelled of sickness.

I tried to wonder how this place once used to be the sheen of India's greatest rulers and home to some of the finest cultures of our people. The beauty of the vestige of a vanished era was now shadowed by anachronism. Look at it today and it portrays only a cross-section of this country's breath-taking poverty. Where was all this poverty when I gazed at it from our boot camp in the hills?

The heat of the morning had risen to settle on the back of my neck and brow. I crossed lane after lane of children on their way to school, merchants opening up their shops, and women and men on their way to work. Most people just walked. After another few minutes of walking, I realized that the side of the street I was now passing through was quite different from the one I'd crossed ten minutes back. The white boat-shaped caps on the heads of the men were replaced by round caps made of net-like fabric. People with bearded faces and women veiled in burqa started to pass by in large numbers. I understood that my first assumption about this place was correct. This was a Muslim neighbourhood.

The street became narrower with every step until it was reduced to the width of a by-lane. The crowd was thicker and it was now beginning to form around me. I felt as if I had accidentally squeezed my body inside a bee hive of human beings and animals. Both sides of the lane were jammed with hovels on whose outsides skin shredded from goats and cows were hanging in the sun and open spaces with mounds of suppurating scat and garbage vans. It gave off a nauseating smell and choked me. I took out a napkin and covered my mouth. People on the lane cast hard glances at me- a man wearing a yarn dyed Arrow shirt and Blackberry trousers with shinning brown shoes trying to navigate the disorder on the streets, without colliding with anyone, like a bat in darkness.

In the course of this not-so-fascinating excursion, I might have taken a few wrong turns somewhere, I thought. I stopped at one point, looking for someone I could ask for directions.

Right at that point, my left knee seemed to be stuck to something. I tried pulling my leg away at first without looking but it had no effect. Upon looking down, I got an instant shock: a goat holding my trousers in between its teeth and grinding at it, thinking it to be some kind of food. I jerked my leg hoping to push it away but she was adamant. To my embarrassment, another goat came running at me and joined her. This one also started chewing the cloth near my knee. Seeing the shape of his horns, I did not dare to push him out of my way. Mortified and helpless, I stood there, looking like a kitten up on a tree, as people watched me.

"I am sorry. These people got out of hand."

A scrawny old man, half-bent by the weight of his hunchback, came walking towards me in hasty steps. He rescued me from his animals and apologized again.

I felt relieved and thanked him.

"Are you new in this area? I haven't seen you here before."

I said I am looking for the school.

"Can you take me there?"

He asked me to follow him.

We passed through a few more gullies with this man and his goats on both sides. Each vennel looked so similar in its appearance and poorness to the one before that I believe even if I did know the roads, it would not require me any special exercise of willpower to get lost here.

On the way, the man asked me where I was from.

"You have come from so far! What are you doing here? Do you have a job?"

"I have come here to teach in this school."

"You look like very young. How far have you studied?"

I said I was an engineering graduate. He stopped and stared at me in astonishment.

"You should be doing something better with your life. You should be building your future. Why are you wasting your time in this neighbourhood?"

I smiled at him.

In the meanwhile, I tried distressfully to form a mental image of a school located in the confines of this sempiternal labyrinth of deformity. I remembered the majestic quietness of my own school, its stately dome ringed by a series of imposing Corinthian pillars. Its chapel, its playground, auditorium and morning prayers all flew before my eyes like an illustrated fairy tale. Yet I was here now in an environment that elicited only awe. How could a place like this, so replete with filthiness and garbage, be a fit site for a school?

I believe I walked for another ten minutes before I finally found my destination behind a vegetable market. A ten feet wall separated a dozen vegetable vendors and another two dozen yelling buyers. A line of people were urinating against this wall. I walked towards its rust-covered brown gate and pushed it aside. It instantly gave out a ear-cracking scream of distress as if I had pushed it open after many years of neglect. This was the front side of the school.

Yet no sooner I had taken my first few steps inside the compound than the high-tide of my enthusiasm receded: I had come inside an abandoned house that looked as if it had been burned down by fire several times. The building was in the shape of an "L". A small rectangular field, which could not have been more than twenty yards on one side and ten on the other, lay adjacent to it. The field had no grass; instead, it was filled with broken pieces of glass, tiles, cement, rubbish, scrap iron, bricks and heaps of paper, plastic bags, containers and garbage. I wondered how so much trash could have come here. There was a lamp post on one side of the gate that had tilted and was gently resting against the wall. On all sides, the building was guarded by electric posts with their wires dropping down from lack of tautness, like cobwebs over my head. On the roof of the building I could see two girls hanging wet clothes upon a rope and wondered if there was a family that lived up there.

Do I have to teach for the next two years in this mess? What have I got myself into?

"Fuck," I said to myself, "I should have taken that job at Infosys."

But there was no looking back now. Bracing myself for the unknown, I entered the building. The corridor on the ground floor stretched about thirty feet with wooden doors running all along its length. The doors were separated by segments of brick walls, hardly three hands in length, with no paint on them. Some of the doors were locked from the outside but some others opened into dark rooms with a few benches. One of the doors carried the plate 'OFFICE' on its outside. I pushed it and walked in. There wasn't much of a decor except a pedestal upon which a small bronze idol of goddess Saraswati was kept. Just opposite the idol, a dusty portrait of Swami Vivekananda was hung from the wall. He was staring at the school's state in dismay. There was no one inside. I looked at the old clock inside in the room. It was 45 minutes past 7 and I was late.

I was told that Mahadeo Govind Ranade School did not have a principal. I was going to meet the teacher who had been acting as the person in-charge in the office of the principal. Mrs Khan was a bulky young woman, perhaps in her early thirties. Her left leg was slightly shorter than the right, which made her walk by dragging her feet. Seeing me, she hurried forward to ask my name.

"I was told you are supposed to come", she said.

I noticed that her English was broken. For every word she spoke in English, she attempted to repeat herself clearly in Hindi. I showed her the papers I had with me, and she wrote down my name in a register and asked me to wait. A woman came in. Must be a peon, I thought. She asked me if I was the new teacher in the school. She said it in Marathi first, then repeating it over in Hindi.

"Yes, I am." I replied in Hindi.

"You do not know Marathi. Am I right?" She exclaimed, in Hindi.

I nodded my head which made her burst out in laughter.

"How are you going to teach then?"

I was quite embarrassed by her words. Isn't this an English-medium school? She went out of the office door, still laughing loudly, and shared the joke with another woman.

"A new teacher has come here and he cannot speak a word of Marathi," I heard her saying out loud. I could not hear what the other woman said except for their muffled laughs.

Mrs Khan came out after ten minutes and apologized for keeping me waiting.

"Let me introduce you to the teachers first and then I will put you in your class."

She took me up the staircase though mounds of dust and shoe-steps of mud. It seemed that the layers of mud had permanently been imprinted on the steps, giving the appearance of an abstract painting. We reached the corridor on the upper floor. The whole corridor was slightly brighter than the one below but dirtier. It was littered with plastic bags, paper balls and empty bottles of Coca Cola. There were one or two flower pots here and there but without the flowers.

On the way, Mrs Khan boasted about all kinds of facilities that the school had and how other schools in the neighbourhood were envious of it.

"Since the day I took over the administration, the school has been running very well. No other school in this neighbourhood can come close. You are fortunate that you will have everything at your disposal."

We entered the first classroom along the corridor. The door was open and I saw a teacher seated in his chair, reading a newspaper. The classroom was filled with so many students that I lost count after a few rows of students. They chatted among themselves in a surly manner, quite oblivious of the fact that they were sitting in a school. Some of the boys had gathered at the window, excitedly trying to get a glimpse of something interesting outside. Upon seeing Mrs Khan, they ran back to their seats.

"He is Mr Gaikwad," Mrs Khan introduced. Mr Gaikwad raised his eyes to look at me and then lowered them into the newspaper again.

"Which class is this?" I asked her.

"Class five," Mrs Khan replied.

We came out of this classroom and entered the next one. Mr Kenjale was teaching here. This time, I introduced myself as the new teacher for the seventh grade and shook his hands.

Mr Kenjale took out a small red box and took out tobacco leaves from it. He began to rub the tobacco leaves in his left palm with his thumb and said, "Oh you will have a tough time with them." he turned his eyes towards Mrs Khan and said, "Only yesterday, those rogues beat a girl in my class and cracked her forehead. We have to do something about this classroom. They are just getting out of our hands day after day."

Turning towards me again, he said "You are new here. So do not hesitate to use the stick if you cannot keep them under control. It is the only language they understand." Mr Kenjale had finished preparing his tobacco. He put the tobacco under his tongue and yelled at his students in a threatening way. I walked out with Mrs Khan, little horrified.

Mrs Khan accompanied me through two more classrooms which had no teachers in them, only students. She explained that the teachers in these classrooms had been transferred but new appointments to fill the vacancies were yet to be made. Some of the existing teachers were acting as substitutes in turns but today there was none.

Just then the peon came running from behind.

"*Medam*, the superintendent has come to meet you in the office."

"I am coming in five minutes. Ask him to wait in the office"

"No he says he is in a hurry. He will leave right now. He only needs some signatures"

"Okay, I am coming down."

Mrs Khan turned to me and pointing at the last door said, "That is your classroom. You can go in."

The last words had come out of her mouth with great affability and a big smile as she went away in steady steps. I would have wanted her to introduce me to the classroom but there was nothing I could do now. She had left me in the lurch. I stood there alone and stared at the door, summoning all my strength.

As I ambulated towards the bend of the "L", I crossed two classrooms that were closed from the outside and headed slowly towards the last door, almost pushing my feet against the floor. With every step that I took, I felt the sweat sinking down through my hair and dripping onto my shoulders. This was not the fear of an entrance examination. This was not the fear of an interview. This was a fear of fear. Like Macbeth terrified by the dagger of the mind. Like Roberto Baggio taking his penalty kick at the World Cup finals.

From a distance, a flux of hoots and snorts were audible. It grew with every step I took forward until I finally entered the room. My eyes widened. Only about ten feet in length and twenty in width, the room was wrapped up with some eighty odd students who were in complete disarray.

Trying to peer in from the outside, I saw several boys and girls standing upon the benches. They were trying to get a glimpse of two hostile girls in the middle of the classroom scrambling to stab each other with scissors while the rest of the class spurred them with a trumpet of slangs.

I immediately tugged through a bunch of rambunctious spectators to reach the scene of the crusade.

"*Teri maa ki...*," one of attackers yelled and spat at the other girl's face.

I tried to pull the attacker aside with both my hands when the other girl threw a flint at my face. It hit me straight at the corner above my left eye and everything became black in an instant. The impulse of the attack was so sudden that I covered my eyes with both my hands and as soon as I did that, I felt my fingers getting wet. A thin stream of blood was oozing through the gap between my fingers. My vision still nitrified by the force of the encounter, my whole body careened out of control for a few seconds when I felt a pair of hands push me from behind. I lurched forward and my head struck against the hard ground.

When I regained consciousness, I saw Mrs Khan sitting before me. I was in her office lying on my back on a bench. There were two other women around me. They held a handkerchief full of ice against my eyes. From what they said, I understood that there was no first-aid kit in the school and I was lucky that they got ice from an ice-cream seller who was crossing the school gate at that time.

Mrs Khan smiled at me.

"I am sorry for what happened," she said trying to comfort me.

I could barely speak. The papers I had brought with me, which contained my lessons plans, were lying at the corner of her table. They had been stamped with the shoes of children. I stared at them blankly. My head was still reeling and the corner of my eye had become black with pain.

Somebody got me a cup of tea. It was black and bitter, and tasted like a medicine.

"It happened very fast," I said very slowly.

"These accidents sometimes happen in our school," she snatched my thought away. "This is a government school after all. You cannot expect these children to be sober. They do not come from families like yours or mine, do they? They come from slums, after all. You would have to be more careful when you are in class. That room has ninety five students and they don't like each other for some reason. That's why they are so notorious. But don't worry, you will get used to this very soon."

My heart skipped a beat. Seeing that I was pale, Mrs Khan assumed that I hadn't yet recovered from the shock. So she decided to give me further explanations.

She continued in a nonchalant voice, "You see, Sir, we have a slight problem in our school. We have over five hundred students from the primary upto upper primary. But some of the classrooms are very old and not in good condition. We cannot teach in those rooms until we get the money to repair them. It's dangerous for everyone. So we are using the same room for two different classrooms. Now, you have sixty students in your classrooms and the other grade, the sixth, has thirty. So it will not be an easy task. I can understand that. We will try to see if we can give you an entire classroom to teach but for the time being, the sixth class students will also sit in your class. If you need any help do not hesitate to call us. I will always be only two doors away, teaching the fourth grade classroom."

This time, my heart swelled with disappointment, and my face looked like the distended belly of a starving cow. I sat there dumbstruck, helpless and despaired. I thought I had hit against a heavy rock and fell head first onto the hard ground. I felt trapped in this place. For months, I had dreamed my classroom to bear a romantic feel, like a garden of infinite innocence and beauty whose trees would bear the fruits of knowledge and the soil would bear the elixir of life. In its cradle children would meet and play. That picture of elegance and serenity had now contracted into a narrow room of unwholesomeness and savagery. Regretting my failed sense of imagination, I tried to conceive the disturbing scene of ninety children sitting in one claustrophobic, airless classroom. I was stirred by that image.

"Shit just got real for me," I thought.

Mrs Khan was waiting for me to ask her anything else I wanted to know. "Do they have a class teacher?" I asked.

"Their class teacher is on leave."

Mrs Khan paused again and thought for a while. "I think you should visit a doctor and take some rest today. You can start teaching from tomorrow."

Before I left, I asked Mrs Khan if she had the curriculum and textbooks. She had none.

When my headache had lessened later in the evening, I riveted my attention into preparing myself for the first real day of teaching. I had poured over a dozen books by educationists and blogs on the internet, since the beginning of summer, grasping the many tested strategies to excellent teaching. This was followed by weeks of hard-work, training and feedback at Teach For India's boot camp that had made me feel sure-footed and strong. I had been trained to understand and tackle the different kinds of learning weaknesses that children of different age groups face. I was equipped with ample resources and lesson plans to give a head start with the children. I had six distinct combinations of dictionary words carefully graded to improve the speaking ability of first-time English language learners. I had planned to teach about five to ten such words every week and thematically mingle them with other forms of language development skills such as writing and speaking. Besides, I had set of comprehension passages, essays and grammar books. To teach mathematics easily, I followed a standardized course catalogue outlining twenty five essential skills that children must master during the year. I had broken down these concepts into a set of easy-to-understand objectives and coupled them with assignments of varying difficulty and skill level.

Yet today was different. There was no confidence but only fear as I tried to wrestle in my head all the odds set against me. The pounding of my head and reeling of my mind made me ask again and again, "How will I protect myself tomorrow?"

There was a daunting challenge ahead of me. I knew that tomorrow I must enter this war-torn classroom not with any imposing pedantic pretension but with the simple conviction that I should be able to teach a lesson for thirty minutes without another brick being thrown at me. I constantly prayed to God, albeit after many years, leaving my river of destiny in his hands.

But the accumulation of my own helplessness and tensions was also overshadowed by an element of deeper concern for the boys and girls I had just witnessed. I wondered what kinds of families and neighbourhoods they came from, how terrific they were from inside and how one could make them learn most efficaciously in an environment most unfit for learning. Sitting there with a pencil in my hand, I realized something that evening that no book or blog had told before: that I must create an environment that will give my students what they needed most- the time and the space to think deeply about their own selves and make meaning out of their experiences. On the one hand, I wanted to evoke their interest in everything- from books, literature and science to sports, music and drama- and replace their empty minds with an open one, but on the other, I wanted them to grow fully by giving them the freedom to express themselves and to explore the world on their own. It is the only way I believed they could find out where they really belonged.

But after several otiose attempts to put my ideas into paper, I gave up. What I did prepare however was a very simple plan and a lot of examples.

TWO

The American novelist Gail Godwin once said, "Good teaching is one-fourth preparation and three-fourths theatre." I learned the truth in this pithy saying when I found myself standing before a class with ninety pairs of eyes looking at me as if I was about to be sentenced by a judge after a murder trial. It was my second day. I took a moment to acclimatize myself with this room. My eyes moved slowly from one side to the other. The whole room must have been not more than twenty feet long on both sides and about fifteen feet in height. The walls were darkened with patches and dampened by rain water seeping from small crevices. The damage to the walls had run so deep that the paint was peeling off at several places. The bricks on the walls were bare. On a few of them, cement was applied. I looked up and saw an artwork of cobwebs hanging from the ceiling.

The classroom had two windows, one on the right and one on the left. The right one was closed but the left was partly opened. There were only two rows of benches in the entire classroom, each row had three benches. The rest of the classroom was empty without any furniture- no fan and only one tube-light. The colour of the blackboard was not black but white-and-grey. It had a big crack in the middle, which could not have but resulted from someone throwing a very heavy object at the board.

"Was the previous teacher in the classroom also attacked?" I thought.

There were boys and girls of all shapes, sizes and colours. Some had come in school uniforms; perhaps others did not have them. The girls from the Muslim community wore burqa. I counted them, they were eighteen. The benches had space enough for only two children to sit but four had managed to squeeze themselves. The rest of the children were sitting on the floor in the aisles between those rows. Every empty space was filled with a child's arm or leg. There was absolutely no way one could reach the back of the classroom once everyone was in their place.

The whole room smelled of urine and sewage. My breath choked. It was unbearable. Is this what a government school was like? How can we even allow children to study in a place like this? More disturbing thoughts crossed my mind and seared my consciousness, while the poison of this place dissolved in my bloodstream faster than sugar in milk. I felt certain that the angel of death was hovering above my head. In a moment, I became incapacitated, and then numb. Today however the children were calm, but not repentant. The two girls whom I had seen yesterday were sitting diagonally opposite each other. They must have recognized who I was from the bandages on my forehead.

For six months before I had come here, I had been possessed by thoughts about what are the things I am going to do once I get here. How am I going to introduce myself to the children? What activities would I plan for them? All these different things had crossed my mind a million times. Little of that excitement subsisted now when I realized that I was going to teach this one classroom for five and a half hours every day, that I was now inextricably trapped in this godforsaken wildness and pestilential stench for the next two years of my life. There was no respite. The very thought of it had wakened me up from sleep three times in the previous night. Haunted by the repeated nightmare of the day gone by, I had dashed very early in the morning, with scorpions crawling in my bellies, so that I do not get lost in the slums of the Peth again.

Since the school had not provided any guidelines, I was quite free to teach whatever I felt like and as a starting point, I had chosen verbs because it was one of those things that I knew well enough when I was a student myself. My lesson was designed in three parts, starting with a general introduction to the idea of time and tenses, shifting to their application in sentences and ending with a set of questions for practice. I had written down all my notes on a separate paper and on the margins of my lesson plan, gathered sufficient materials and thought of a couple of activities to keep the children engaged in the class work. But while my goal for the children was to begin tenses, I had set a far more pressing goal for myself: I must succeed in my lesson today. Like Napolean lost in the battle of Waterloo, the failure on the previous day had struck a hard blow to my authority as a teacher and I desperately wanted to regain control.

Having taken a painstaking look at my classroom, I took out my plan from my pocket. For a few minutes, I stared dully at it. Then I looked up and gazed at the faces of the children, motionless, and waiting. Their eyes were riveted to my own. Suddenly I felt a sting of pity through my heart and a burst of tears filled my inner eyes. "What the hell am I doing? My lessons will make no sense to these children," I said to myself.

I carefully put my lesson plan inside my pocket and tried to clear my throat. I remembered what my mother, one of the most scintillating story-tellers I knew, had once told me: "Keep narrating and ideas will come."

"Today," I said, ratcheting up my volume. "I am going to tell you a story about a journey I made many years ago into one of the forests of India. The name of this forest is Sunderban and it located along the coast of the Bay of Bengal. The forest has got its name from a very special tree which is called the Sundari tree. Sundari means beautiful. The Sunderban forests are spread over the delta of the river Ganga, India's largest river. The Sunderban is full of small rivers and water bodies which are connected to every corner of the forest.

"Several predators live in the labyrinth of the channels, branches and roots that poke up into the air. You will find monkeys, apes, birds, leopards, bison, deer, mugger-much, lizards and snakes. But there is one animal that is considered the King of the Sunderaban. He is called the Royal Bengal Tiger and he oversees the whole jungle. All the other animals are afraid of him. When I was of your age, I had gone on an adventure trip with my family to the Sunderbans. Today, I am going to tell you what I saw there.

"We went in a large steam boat along the river Ganga. For four days, we stayed on the waters in our boat and reached the marshlands. Forests of Sundari trees stood on both sides of the river. They have a thick canopy.

"We reached a village on the banks of the river. The people of this village are fisherman but some of them also work as honey collectors. Their village was very close to a place where one hundred tigers lived!

"On our first night, we were welcomed by the villagers who celebrated our visit with dances and music. The villagers worship a folk goddess named BanBiwi. They told us the story of Ibrahim of Medina who was blessed by the Archangel Gabriel, to be the father of twins. The girl was named BanBiwi and her brother Shah Jangli. When they became adults, they were sent by the Archangel to the shores of Sunderbans, where a demon named Dakkin Roy ruled and terrorized human beings. BanBiwi and Shah Jangli vanquished the powerful Dakkhin Roy and saved the humans. Then BanBiwi divided the country into two parts, one protected by her where the humans could live and one still reigned by Dakkin Roy. The villagers went to work every day after taking her blessing. They believed that if the goddess blessed them, then they would return safely from the jungles. Otherwise they would be attacked by the tigers or eaten by a mugger-much that lived on Dakkin Roy's land.

"In that village lived an old man named Khalid Miya who was one of the honey collectors in the Sunderbans. He had to go to the forests once a month to search for honey. The hives were located deep inside the forests. When he went inside, his family member in the village kept praying to Allah for his life. He carried several weapons under his shirt- axe, knives and daggers. He covered himself with mud all over his body so that the tiger would not be able to see him in the jungle. When he reached the hive, he put a cloth all over his face and held a burning torch near the hive. The smoke filled the air quickly and the bees, thinking that the jungle is on fire, decided to discard their hive and flee. Once the bees leave, Khalid would cut the hive safely and return with pure gold, which he would sell every Saturday in the markets.

"Khalid Miya and his son Irfan had a country boat. One day, before sunrise, they were preparing for their travel into the jungle, sitting on their boat that was anchored on the bank of the dark misty river. They could not see anything. Khalid Miya was behind Irfan with his back to the bank. Suddenly Irfan heard a strange sound and turned back. He saw a tiger had leaped out of the bushes and grabbed his father by the neck. His heart became cold in fear. He did not even have a weapon or a lathi with him. But he wasted no time. He picked up the mud from the shore and hurled it into the tiger's eyes, blinding it momentarily. The demon was shocked and stepped back, releasing Khalid Miya's neck. As it tried to get the mud off its eyes, Irfan lifted his father onto the boat and began to row away as fast as he could.

"He told us more stories about the tiger. When a tiger crosses the jungle, it gives off a smell. This smell is intercepted by none other than monkeys who start screeching immediately. The deer and bison which roam in the neighbourhood have special ears to hear the scream of the monkeys and they understand that a tiger is nearing the area. Even the villagers could interpret this sound very well when they went inside the jungle.

"In the Sunderbans, the water was salty. In all other habitats, tigers drink fresh water. It is believed that the saltiness of the water in this area has put them in a state of constant discomfort, leading them to be extremely aggressive. When the fishermen go to fish, they put on a masks made to look like faces of men to wear on the back of their heads because tigers always attack from behind. The high tides in the area destroy the tiger's urine which they use as territorial markers. Thus, the only way for a tiger to defend its territory is to physically dominate everything that enters. These tigers have grown used to human flesh due to the weather. Cyclones in this part of India kill thousands, and the bodies drift out in to the swampy waters, where tigers scavenge them. The villagers believed that tigers find hunting animals difficult due to the continuous high and low tides making the area marsh-like and slippery. Humans travel through the Sundarbans on boats gathering honey and fish, making for easy prey. They said that when a person stops to work, the tiger mistakes them for an animal.

"We travelled through the forests on our boat with the villagers. One of the villagers knew the deepest tributaries of the marshlands by the back of his hand. The forest officers often hired him to put collars around the necks of tiger. When we had reached deep, we saw the golden black dragon the jungle. We were in the water, it was on the land. It was only two hundred metres away. It must have been seven feet in length and its tail was more than three feet long. It must have been about two hundred and fifty kilograms in weight. It was wearing a red collar in its neck. The tiger was eating flesh from a dead deer. Blood was all over its mouth. Just as our boat took a turn and came slightly near the animal, its eyes fell upon us and it roared loudly. The whole jungle seemed to shake in fear. Then it leaped and vanished into the wild."

I took a long breath when I had finished. I had spoken for half an hour, trying to narrate as much as I could remember. I had spoken in Hindi, for none could comprehend English properly. The sixth class did not have any teacher coming in for the day, so they had no other option but to listen to my story quietly. All through the time, I had been noticing and monitoring every movement of the children in utter awe but to my great delight, not even one of them moved from their places for once. I felt vindicated that I had overcome my fears without committing any of the cardinal sins of teaching.

For the rest of the day, the children did not create any serious calamity in the classroom. Besides nattering with each other, they were reasonably well-disposed. It made me feel a lot more comfortable about myself and in control of the situation.

At about eleven in the morning, the peon came to my classroom with another man and asked me to vacate the classroom.

"Medam has asked us to run a curtain through the middle of the room," he said. "Your class will sit on this side of the curtain and the sixth grade class on the other. Medam said that we cannot keep them together."

He drove the children out of the classroom onto the hallway like a cattleman. Then he got up on a stool and drilled two holes on opposite walls and fit a steel rod through it. He then dragged a red curtain from the office upto the room. The curtain had no hooks, so he tied it to the rod with nylon ropes. When the curtain stood up, I saw several hundred holes in it, some of them big enough to push a child's head through. The room however was immediately reduced to half its size, even though there were more thirty more children in my class than the other. The children filed into their respective compartments like chicken in a poultry.

The peon came again after the break to see if everything was okay. He informed that Mrs Khan had called all the teachers to the office for a staff meeting. Incidentally, this meeting was the only staff meeting we had in the course of the entire academic year. Keeping in tune with the narrative I had shared in the class, I asked the children to take out their notebooks and write a composition on a memorable adventure they have had in life. Placing that load of work, I was quite contended that children would remain occupied for the remaining part of the day.

In the office, I counted the number of teachers in the school. Besides three teachers who were absent on that day, we were seven in number- four female teachers and six male teachers in all. Clearly, we were outnumbered by a huge margin by the six hundred odd children.

Mrs Khan spoke for most of the time and the teachers listened quietly. She first read out a few norms and regulations from a printed document which had been sent to the school to guide us through the recently-legislated Right to Education Act. Then she discussed the most acute problem facing the school, that of proper toilets. The school did not have separate toilet for the girls and this had become a menace for the parents. After much deliberation, Mrs Khan had put a tall heap of bricks and sacs to divide the main toilet into two, in the same way as she divided my classroom. The teachers did not have any toilet facility. Two female teachers were present in the meeting and they pressed hard for the toilet. Mrs Khan promised that she would look into the matter. She also assigned a list of responsibilities to the teachers. I was put in charge of the extra-curricular activities in the school.

It was decided that Ms Zareen and Ms Aliya will assist me in preparing the students for Independence Day, Teacher's day, Savitri Bai Phule's birth anniversary, Dr Ambedkar Jayanti and finally our Annual Concert. I was glad to be given this big responsibility so early. Mrs Khan reiterated that all teachers needed to come regularly to school so that these events could be pulled off.

"Don't tell me later on that you did not have any time." Mrs Khan lamented and chided in the same tone, "The concert has been cancelled three years in a row. I have received complaints from the authorities. They say that your teachers are all *nikammah*. So this year, we all have to buckle up in order to save our face."

The meeting was over in half an hour and we walked back to our classes. On the staircase, Mrs Khan jokingly congratulated me because I had not cracked my head once again.

Upon coming back, I found to my disappointment that only two of the children had completed their work while others had scribbled just a word or two or written only their names on paper. I collected the papers one by one and put them carefully inside my bag, trying to put up a façade about how serious I was about their assignments and school work. It was not so important, I thought. Inside my heart, I was grateful and overjoyed that my real first day had gone quite well and I kept thinking of how I am going to make a small celebration at home to observe my success. But little did I know then that this would be the first and the last day in the three-month long period when I was able to achieve what I had in mind.

THREE

It is always the little things around us that often unveil the most genuine picture of our past, present and perhaps our future. In our school, it was an old name plate, which was hanging loosely in the vestibule from two of its ends only. The screws of the other two ends had fallen out of the bores ever since the school's reputation and prosperity had precipitated into a toxic cocktail of sheer discredit and perpetuating failure. The name of the school, which had once been etched with pride upon the plate in golden letters, had slowly withered away to an almost unassuming single alphabet- the last standing witness to the school's abysmal fall from grace.

There were four different government schools imparting instructions in three different mediums that shared the building of Mahadeo Govind Ranade. During the morning, the school premises hosted the English medium unit and the co-educational Urdu medium and in the afternoon, the premises belonged to the Marathi medium school and an all-girls Anglo-Arabic school. Classes on the west half of the corridor belonged to the English medium school and those on the north side were of the Urdu medium. There was only five feet gap in between through which the staircase ran. A collapsible gate separated the two schools.

The English medium unit was the newest addition to the building. It was established only fifteen years ago by two teachers. Their efforts materialized into establishing the nursery section of the school. In those days, the idea of attending an English-medium school was not pervasive. It was something that people in a poor neighbourhood associated with the upper class elitism that they lacked. Initially, people in the neighbourhood were scared to put their children there. In the first year, only fifty students enrolled in the English-medium, only twenty one among them came from the neighbourhood. All of the children who had taken admission were boys. There were only two classrooms and the two teachers who had started the school taught in English. In the second and third year, however, the excitement about the new watermark in the school which was the English-medium had doubled. The school's strength reached a hundred and sixty students. There were still two classrooms and three teachers managed them.

Gradually the school grew its primary and secondary divisions, adding seven more teachers and more than five hundred students. The number of classrooms however had not grown proportionately to the number of students. There were only seven rooms available, one among them was remodelled into the office and the other was a storeroom. There was only one extra room, which was named as the Hall room, only because it was a little larger than the rest of the rooms. Students in the first and second grade were put there. One of the classrooms sat on the rear side of the Hall and the other sat on the front side.

Ever since the English-medium was established, the Urdu-medium school had witnessed a decline in its enrolments while admissions in the English-medium school far exceeded its capacity. The growing presence of the English medium in the same building had also dealt a strong blow to its reputation in the neighbourhood. Many parents had taken their children out of Urdu medium and put them in English medium and this general disinclination of the neighbourhood towards the Urdu-medium had however greatly discomforted its teachers, and to a lesser extent the teachers of the Marathi-medium section. This in turn irked them to occasionally trouble us and make it impossible for us to teach.

Besides the obvert difference in the design of their uniforms, there was no significantly perceptible difference in the poorness of education that each of the schools offered. One did not have to strain his eyes to see what was happening. Children sat in classrooms idly, with no work to do other than picking at each other. Either there was no teacher in the classroom at all or the teacher was shooting the breeze in the office with the other teachers. One teacher spent over half his day talking over his mobile phone. The woman on the other side of the conversion was another teacher to whom this teacher recently got engaged. In Mrs. Khan's own classroom, no activity was taking place. She remained submerged under the weight of a truckload of papers, forms and registers that would come from the government department.

In the seventh standard, there were sixty students- forty one boys and nineteen girls. I had thirty eight Muslim students, thirteen girls and twenty five boys, and twenty two Hindus, six girls and sixteen boys. Several of them had been struggling to pass for years. Others were still struggling to fit into the environment of a school and so far had only managed to earn the opprobrium of the teachers who thought that these children were no better than street thugs.

In my case, their infamy transpired through a visible sentiment of intolerance. Almost every child was disinterested in whatever I was trying to teach. Almost every one of them would be talking, laughing, hitting or yelling at each other for no real reason whatsoever. Their feelings for me came to rest somewhere between comical amusement and outright rejection. For a first time teacher, it was painful and insulting to go through such conspicuous absence of display of inquisitiveness about the subject matter of any of my lessons and I had no choice but to keep experimenting with different ideas on how to teach in a manner that would make lessons more interesting. Often in the week, I came up with rib-tickling and risible classroom antics to draw the attention of my students towards my lessons, but nothing really seemed to favour me.

My own foolishness however was insignificant to the bigger problem I had in my hand. A large number of children in my classroom were barely able to read or write a word in English. Some of them still could not spell or write their names correctly. In the six years of their school life gone by, they had only managed to memorize a handful of words, consisting of not more than two alphabets and even fewer three-lettered words. Their otherwise loud voices would asphyxiate into mildness until no more broken words or sounds would come out of them. Naturally, teaching them to understand any of the other subjects such as history, geography and science was beyond the confines of human capacity because their books were written in the language they feared most. In mathematics, the class's overall skill set had paused at addition without carry-overs and subtraction without borrowing. Last year the classroom did not have a teacher for even a single working day and in the previous years, the teachers had not paid much attention. If one looked at them, one would not know whether to cry or complain. One would not even know where to start from. I kept asking myself, "Where would they go forward from here?" My nerves jittered to find an answer.

The school hours lasted from seven in the morning to twelve in the afternoon. But a teacher would have been considered lucky if he could manage to teach in a class until after nine in the morning. There was a shed right underneath my classroom where tyres were burnt every morning and the smokes would engulf the entire classroom. My classroom, that now resembled a small confined prison cell, became unusually hot and awfully suffocating. The other window had to be kept closed all the time just to avoid the stink of urine and excreta from transuding into our classroom.

Right opposite the shed on the side, where the slums stood, was a small garage where a generator and a grinding machine operated simultaneously, making a noise so deafening that would it cause any sane-minded person to lose concentration after every two minutes. Countless precious hours of teaching simply vanished like puffs of smoke this way. There was one more nuisance that seemed impossible to contain. It was the fear of rats. Two giant rats, which were as big as cats, lived in the drain pipes and could easily creep into our classrooms. They preyed upon the tiny kids of the schools by chomping the flesh off their legs.

From nine onwards, the disruption both outside and inside in the classroom rose to a decibel louder than a harvest thunderstorm. There was a classroom right next to our room. In this room, third standard students were seated. The teacher would come a little before nine and ask the children to repeat multiplication tables from two till fifteen. The children yelled in chorus, "two ones are two, two twos are..." This went on like a routine exercise, every single day of the week. The children across the hallway slapped the tables and benches so blatantly that there was no way I could make myself audible beyond the first three or four rows of my classroom. Seeing that I was incapacitated, students in my own classroom would quickly join the rest of the school band's competition to earn the reputation for the loudest hoots and hisses. The air soon came to be filled with the abuses describing one another mothers and fathers. No form of control or discipline could quieten them.

The noise was accompanied by a bunch of boisterous loitering boys who would peep in through the door of my classroom and make whistles. As soon as I took notice, I would run at them to shoo them away. Then they came up with a prank that they played religiously, at least twice every day. A group of children came to my door and banged on the door but before I could reach the door to see who the culprit was, they raced away. This would generate a counter storm of hasty-powder-fired slangs and rude humour that would take my innermost self into a grappling hold. How was it possible for such young boys to be conditioned this way even before they are able to reason?

While I had established a rule that no student would hurl slangs at another, it did not really have any effect on them. I had to keep reminding the children a dozen times every day that they were not following the rule. When that failed, I tried instituting severe penalties against those using slangs, which included informing the principal or getting their parents to school. Some had calmed down after one or two visits to Mrs Khan's room, but some were beyond my reach. One Asif in my class declared an open war against me, "I don't care where you people find your bullshit morals from. All lies. I hate you as much as I hate all these mongrels here."

My introduction with Asif was completed when I found him in a roughshod fight with a student from the Urdu medium. A gang of boys barged into my classroom after the break time to seek for Asif. I interfered but they asked me to stay out of this.

"This is our own private matter. We will settle it ourselves."

That day after school, Asif was severely beaten up by two senior boys, including the one who had lost his money, in his locality. I informed Mrs Khan immediately.

"Let them do whatever they want. They will not stop until they kill them." The next day, I found him with his chin bandaged and other bruises on his arms. His nose and three fingers of his left hand were also broken from that fight. He confessed how the boys had followed him on his way back from school and then dragged him to a narrow alley to work over him.

Asif's family was settled in a slum in Mangalwar Peth. His real mother had died when he was only four years old.

She had learned that her husband had secretly married a woman in the village with whom he had three sons. Some say that she committed suicide while others claim that his father strangled her to death. After her death, his father was arrested and sent to prison for a while. Since then, Asif had been growing up under the stewardship of his grandmother and uncle.

Unfortunately for them, his father had left behind no monetary means to support his upbringing. His uncle and aunt kept torturing him one way or the other, often resorting to whipping and verbal abuse, reducing him to the status of a man servant in his own house. In return, he got some food sometimes twice a day, sometimes only once. When he was not working, he used to go out into the slum and mingle with boys who were fifteen years older than him. Influenced by their companionship, he developed the habit of stealing money from his grandmother's purse to buy whatever those boys had and do whatever they did. This stealing was the reason why he had lost his eye. His uncle had caught him stealing money from the house and had driven a drilling machine in running state through his left eye.

On my third day of school, he attempted to escape from the school premises after the break by climbing over the wall. Fortunately the guard had come for duty that day and had caught him red-handed. He was pulled down by the collar and deposited in my custody.

The lunch break was thirty minutes long. That was the time when the school building would break into bedlam and disorder. Like the Crusades of the Middle Ages. In the minutes leading upto the lunch break my students would be tipping on the cusp of chaos. Their attention resembled a thin wire from which a weight was suspended. The tension in the wire had reached the limit of tolerance. If there was any delay in ringing the bell, the children began shouting and screaming vulgarities at the peon. They started getting up and running around, even encircling me in groups and pushing me to give up so that they could go out. I had no choice in this matter. I felt like a helpless child trying in vain to settle things. If I could calm down that one bunch of rambunctious boys at the right corner of the room, another bunch of girls on the left side would collapse into utter pandemonium. I felt the hopelessness of a child playing passing the ball with a bunch of older boys and girls.

The scene of the lunch continued to upset me deeply for many days. As soon the lunch would reach the school, the students rushed and hurdled all around it with open lunch boxes. Serving over five hundred students took time and every one could not get their share of the mid-day meal before the break time ended. Often I witnessed the scene from the upper corridor- little children getting pushed out of the way by the bigger ones. The little ones however did not give up trying, but kept on nudging their bodies in. Once they secured their lunch, the winners had to now jostle to find some space to sit down in the corridors and eat. The corridors however were shrouded in dust and mud coming from the shoes of students running around recklessly. Some sat on the ground, some on the staircase. Some of the children also got money from their home, a privilege they widely flaunted to their friends for the entire two hours leading up to the lunch break. With a two rupee coin or a five, they rushed outside the school gate to the shops on the other side of the road. Those who lost the fight walked back to class hungry.

Lunch was brought to the school premises every day by a woman who had contracted with the school for this purpose. The recipe was very simple: it comprised of no fruits, no eggs, no bread, no biscuits, but plain rice and dahl. What she served for lunch was anything but nutritious-half-cooked rice and dahl that could be easily mistaken as light yellow-coloured water. Part of the lunch was sent to many of the teachers and peons before it was served upon the children. As for me, I had the honour of sharing in the midday meal only once.

Later that day, the woman who cooked the meal came up to me and said, "Sir, do not eat the food that we serve to the children. It is not good for your health. If you want to have lunch, then tell me. I will get you a special lunch. It will cost you only 40 rupees every day. You can pay me at the end of the month also." I said nothing.

In more than one way, lunch was the most important activity of the day and I learned that for many students, it often summarized the whole purpose of putting on their uniforms. With the exception of two students or so, almost everyone ate part or whole of the meal that was served. This was no surprise because food was a critical shortage for people in these precincts and most of the children had seen days, usually during the end of every month, when there would be no food to eat at home. Almost invariably, they came to school with an empty stomach. Some drank a small cup of tea or a roti left over from the previous night. Fainting was common in the primary classes. There, the hunger was so severe on some days that as the hours progressed, the children would get increasingly restless and aggressive in the classroom, some even holding their stomachs tightly with their two hands, hoping to strangle the pain to death. As I paraded like a clean and immaculate monk through this mess, I was often reminded of the pictures of soldiers starving in the Russian winter of the Great War. Some of these skeleton shaped child soldiers often shared their hungriest confessions, like Parul, a girl from the fourth grade, who said that her mother always advised her to fill herself with as much peat as she could in school so that she would not be hungry until ten in the night. She had innocently admitted to me that her father's drinking habits left them with little to buy ration for the entire family. Being the eldest in her house, she unfailingly filled her tiffin box every day with enough food to take back for her sisters.

If food was a precious gift of the school to its children, water was even rarer to find. There was a water-point near the makeshift bathroom, but all the taps were always dry like a pond in summer. Seldom did a drop travel along the pipes to make it to the finish line, mixed with sewer all along its long winding journey, where a bunch of children fought for its possession. Water was mostly brought from the outside, not for human consumption but for cleaning the school. by two safai karmacharis whose job it was to broom the floors and keep the classes and the corridors clean. Despite that, water had clogged near the bathroom and had become a breeding ground for mosquitoes and flies in the early rains of the monsoon. From morning onwards paper balls, plastic packets, crushed bottles and chunks of dust would lie everywhere on the floors of the classrooms and on the outside and after lunch, the corridors were patterned with crumbs of rice and goblets of dahl and long lines of water.

Being an OCD about cleanliness, I made it a point to patrol the school corridor from end to end in the way a janitor walks around his dungeon. However with only two eyes and two hands, I could not impose discipline as consistently as I desired to but my presence did calm down many of those who went around looking for obvious chances to inject troubles. But there were much more than mere cleanliness that escaped my attention. Vehement fights broke out in the toilets almost every day and students would return to class with bruises on their foreheads and arms. Fights flared up on the field, sometimes in the corridors, sometimes in the classrooms and sometimes on the pavement outside the school gate.

The lunch time certainly brought the school down to a state of half-demented malfunction, as if some spirit with her malefic charm had possessed the children. Few went missing every day after lunch. The same faces usually. They would quietly slip out of the gate by mingling themselves in the crowd. The teachers knew about this but they did not complain. They believed it was always better to have a class with less commotion.

The towers of disruption in my own classroom regularly became twice as aggressive and difficult to control for the two hours they had to stay in school after lunch-time, as if a volcano had erupted under their feet. Noise levels increased, slangs flew by and small local fights broke out. In one of those fights, three children rolled themselves over each other and brought the whole curtain down, tearing the whole thing apart with a whizzing sound. The curtain was replaced with a new one after four long weeks.

Those who remained calm in the morning now became boisterous, like a sleeping giant who had been energized and woken up after his lunch. The first hour after lunch went in trying to get all these hyperactive shavers to sit in their proper places. I ran from one end of the classroom to the other, holding them by their hands to bring them back to their seats. It was in this attempt that I discovered that my own diary was missing from my bag. Three days later, I found it at one corner of my classroom, stabbed and mutilated with compasses and pen-nibs.

The classroom on the other side of the curtain would make things worse for me. Some of them began to play with cards. They placed a red cloth on the floor and three players made a circle around it. Two others were spectators. The rest of the class screeched in a frenzied chorus at each other like wild animals, with their loud voices gurgling in the air, like the galleries of a football match, which made it impossible for my students to hear instructions.

My shirt stuck to my skin glued by sweat. My shoulders became wet under the ceaseless rainfall of the disturbing monsoons. Crazed with panic and gripped by hysteria, I whirled around the classroom, tossing and tumbling. I wanted to tear my hair apart. What was I looking for? Divine intervention, perhaps. I shook my head often like a dog, as flies and mosquitoes pestered me. After the school would get over, I cleaned the entire classroom, picking up the paper balls, wafer packets and clumps of rice and dahl which had been thrown at one another. Yet only the next morning I would find my classroom mucked up with garbage by the children who shared the same classroom in the afternoon shift. They pulled out the planks from the benches to expose the nails and scrawled the blackboard with slangs. Burned-down *bidis* filled the corners of my classroom. I panicked again and again at the site of this mess and the scale of the cataclysm I was exposed to.

My first week of teaching had passed by without even realizing. I felt that in six days, I had done so much and absolutely nothing at the same time- I was overjoyed by my conquests in the classroom and overwhelmed by the depth of work that lay before me.

In this little time, I found myself at the crossroads of a kind of life, quite new to me, that was rushing past me like a hurricane, swaying me in the mayhem of its distorted colours, smells, sounds and its men, women and children. I was absorbing and registering all that I was seeing with wide eyes, not thinking, not examining. But residing just below the surface of my cognition was an inexplicable subconscious understanding and yet a mundane wonder of unimaginable kind that a week of stay in this place had brought to me. This understanding, which I could only feel trilling and paralyzing my brain, had emerged from the tangible signs of squalor and indignity that I had witnessed since coming here. I was afraid how easily I was getting involved in every incident that was taking place in this compound. It had sensitized me. I quickly became calculating and watchful of people and of little things near me. My mind screamed with feelings of anger, desperation and impatience about the future of every child that I was responsible for and the need to demonstrate tolerance and generosity and deep courageousness. I had already begun to see that teaching will not be a mere exercise of dictation and thoughtless imitation of notes and lectures and after a week, I realized that it did not matter how many English words children could spell correctly or whether they could identify rhyme and meter in poetry. As my plans continued to sway from occasional successes to frequent failures every day, the true purport of education only became clearer. I had stumbled against new questions every day, questions that were roadblocks in my way. What did an education really mean to the less advantaged children of this country? What was it object, its means and ends? Into which world would it lead them? For now, I did not know the answers, but hoped that my students will tell me in time.

FOUR

Among the teachers of the school, Mrs Yasmin S was an exception. In her early fifties, she was in the profession for nearly three decades and although she taught in the Urdu-medium, it was her persistent efforts that had led to the establishment of the English-medium school.

Mrs S was the most ebullient and competent teacher I came across in Mahadeo Govind Ranade School, well-disposed and with stoic patience that was complemented by a svelte nature and a sense of humour which could immediately draw anyone in. She was the most experienced teacher in the school but she had continued to remain child-like with a heart full of passion, like an April day. She joked with the young teachers and laughed heartily, keeping the mood light all the time. Although Mrs S had no real authority to make decisions for the school, Mrs Khan greatly admired her wisdom and judgment.

The first time I had met her was during the staff meeting on the second day of school. Since then, she had loved me like her own son. Mrs S taught me how to handle the bullies and ruffians in class. She had some deep intuition in these matters for she had taught all of them when they were younger and therefore understood them very intimately. She would never come to attack them with a stick or even scorn or offend them verbally. That made her very different from the rest of the teachers. Whenever she talked with a tough child, she would slowly put her hand on the child's head in an act of blessing him, in an exceptionally soft and polite way, a distinct kind of treatment that they never expected to see from a teacher. So they feared and respected her at the same, standing with their heads down with shame. As often as I observed this, I made up my mind that I would always send the troublemakers in my class to Mrs S for their cure.

Mrs S had an epileptic student in her class. His name was Omkar. Mrs S's class was often interrupted by his nervous breakdowns and fits. On my fourth day itself, I witnessed Mrs S carrying this boy in her arms towards the office room. His eyeballs could not be seen and his lips had curled up. His mouth was foaming and his whole body was shaking vehemently, like a bled calf. The tremor was so intense that his feet kicked against Mrs S's arm. I dashed immediately towards the office and met Mrs S at the doorstep. She asked if I had a metal key. I took out the house keys from my pocket and she put it inside his fist. I held the boy's arms tightly as she took out his shoes and started rubbing his feet. Within minutes, the *sevikas* came rushing into the office and brought a jar of water. Mrs S hydrated his face by taking the water in her hands.

Omkar recovered after about ten minutes. He opened his eyes but he was barely able to speak. Mrs S asked if his was taking his medicine daily. He said he wasn't. She looked at me in despair.

"His parents don't have money to buy the tablets," she said. "The last time this had happened, I took him to a neurologist and got his tests done. Before that, his parents had taken him to a *baba*, known to cure these fits, who had put rings on his fingers and tied these ribbons on his arm."

Later on the same day, Omkar had fits thrice within an hour's time. His body had melted like a wax candle. We gave him water and orange juices to drink and biscuits to eat until his mother came to school. She started her conversation with a sob that kept on intensifying every time someone in the office offered her a piece of advice about the little boy.

"This is God's curse. What can we do? We are trying everything. We go to the Ganapati temple every week to pray for him. But he is not showing any recovery." Mrs S scolded her for not following the doctor's prescription and asked her to stop her whining. I wondered if she at all listened.

When her wails had dried and she was ready to take her son home, Mrs S took her outside the office gave her five hundred rupees from her purse. No one saw that except me: the insoluble compassion of a teacher for a student, the incomparable legacy of a person that is often what isn't seen. My deference for Mrs S multiplied several times over. I came to regard her in my mind as my guide and mentor and had unwittingly become her student.

Mrs S quickly became my first pillar of support because so far I had only managed to feel helpless about myself. I believe Mrs S knew what the life of a novice teacher was and she never hesitated to advise me on the problems I was facing in the classroom. Among other things, she helped me learn how to cook Maharashtra's delicacies and absorb as much Marathi as I could. She would write down recipes on a piece of paper and hand it over to me. I learned to make *thalipeeth*. It is prepared by mixing rice, atta, besan, rava, ragi and cumin powder along with minced onions and then evenly cooking the dough in oil. The smack of *thalipeeth* when eaten with a dollop of butter has a surprising resemblance to the veridical perception of Maharashtra- earthy and humble, but diverse and delectable, she had told me.

From Mrs S, I also learned about the unforgiving history of the school. She had come to the school in the year 1982. Since then she had been through all the ups and downs of the school and seen its heydays and its subsequent fall to shame. Her memory was extremely sharp and acute- she knew the names of almost every child in the school and she could recognize them immediately.

When she started the English-medium school, Mrs S taught in both divisions- the Urdu-medium and the English-medium- for four years until more teachers were hired.

"We taught in horrible conditions. There were only two classrooms at the time but so many students. There was no toilet for the teachers or the students."

While she said this, I tried to construct a visual image of what the school might have looked like twenty years ago and reconcile that image with the one that I have been seeing for a week. If the situation now can be best described as deplorable, I thought, what might have been the situation when Mrs S had come first. The thought rattled me for a moment.

In my first couple of weeks, the other teachers in the school treated me less amicably than Mrs S. To be honest, they were a little wary of my presence. This might have come from the sense of exclusivity that my florid dressing and fluent English pronunciation had generated in them. I was the only teacher in the entire school who could read, write and speak in English- a privilege that few in the school possessed. I carried a laptop regularly which I used to organize my schedules. They were enamoured by it. Some of them asked me if I could teach them how to use Facebook.

One of the teachers, Mr. Ingale, who taught the first standard classroom, almost always assisted Mrs Khan with all kinds of administrative duties, in the hope that one day he might be elevated to the seat of the principal. Consequently, children in his classroom had been sitting, doing nothing other than slapping their hands on the desks or bickering ferociously with one another. It was decided that three substitute teachers and at other times the *sevikas*, would be coming in turns at regular intervals to monitor the children.

Besides sharing in the general administration, Mr Ingale's also had voluntarily assumed that it was his responsibility to maintain law and order in the school and therefore, he carried a temperament that was scarred by more vanity than all the Guzmans put together. And to make his authority felt, he regularly imposed on the children the most dehumanizing and disgraceful punishments. His victims were however always the most meek and fearful-looking boys and girls.

"You mongrel," I heard him scathe a student in the corridor one day. "Before I come back I want this floor cleaned. You belong to the sweeper caste, sweeping is what you are going to do here."

Mr Ingale also managed to apply his bureaucracy on some of the teachers. As often as possible, he would barge his way into my classroom for his administrative works, bluntly interrupting my lessons. This he did with a buckram conviction that no other business in the classroom could be more important than his. Often he simply came to inspect me. And every time, his entry used to cause such undulations of anxiety for he stared at me with his inexorably hostile eyes that it kept me guessing what I had possibly done to annoy him. However, my students remained unflustered, as always.

Mrs Khan, who constantly worried that I might not be at ease with my gang of troublemakers, asked me a number of times to visit ad observe Mr. Ingale when he took lessons in his class. I had no option but to oblige.

When that fortunate moment arrived after a few weeks, I discovered some unique things in his classroom. In the front were students who were relatively better than the rest in terms of academic outcomes. These students answered questions, wrote down notes correctly and paid attention to him. Towards the back of the class were students who were academically weaker, listless and disinterested in learning. Those in front were boys while those at the back were all the girls and Muslims students.

One can find no logical justification for introducing such a configuration in a classroom other than the fact that he did not think it was his responsibility to address the educational needs of those children who were consistently falling behind others. As I ambulated to the back of the back of the classroom, I saw there were many who couldn't read at all. But happy that he had set the students with an assignment after a fifteen minute English lesson, in which he erred over a dozen times, Mr Ingale left for his official chores.

The weight of his responsibilities indeed created an almost maddening working condition for him, but less exacerbating than the way it affected the learning trajectory of the students. The math average of the class was perpetually below the failing score of 35. The reading and writing were at the third-grade level, a couple of grade levels below. The overall situation in English was too worse to put numerically. Often the parents complained and expressed their discontent but it had no effect whatsoever on the administration's unassailable faith on Mr Ingale or on what was to become of the students.

"Don't talk to these parents at all," Mrs Khan advised me as well. "If they say anything to you, ask them to come to my office. I will deal with them." Unfortunately, the parents were all afraid of meeting Mrs Khan for they believed that she would never summon them unless their children commit something grave to deserve outright punishment. For their children, the cycle of losses thus went unbridled.

There were several other schools in our neighbourhood, none of which were in any way better than my own school. In fact, most were in run-down condition. In an Anglo-Arabic school that stood at about two hundred metres from ours and looked like a woebegone old shack, there was one classroom which had a hundred and six students but only one teacher to manage. On most of the days, the school authorities asked twenty or so students to remain absent. All the desks, tables and chairs had been removed because the furniture was eating up space in the classroom. With that also, the number of students far exceeded the space available and many had to sit outside the door. In another school, which had the same problem, a girl had gone missing.

"Nothing had been done to make the situation any better," said a teacher who had been transferred from that school to ours, "The parents of the school children pressed hard for the school to take quick action, but nothing happened eventually, only students started dropping out in big numbers."

Mahadeo Govind Ranade School also faced many ignominious situations from time to time but what was central to all of its problems was the school administration's perpetual indisposition to recognize that anything was at all a problem. Within a few weeks, my observant nature found out that the school's playground, being a municipal property, was used almost all of the time for civic works rather than for its children. Whenever the municipal corporation repaired roads in the neighbourhood, the construction workers were asked to use the school ground for burning tar. Smoke filled the air and viscid substances sullied the ground. An old building right behind the school, which was at the brink of collapse, was repaired. The masons got bricks, cement and sand to dump onto the ground. Trucks belonging to the municipal corporation would be parked on the ground, making it impossible to let the children be on the ground. There was also an Innova and three or four bikes, all belonging to the local Corporator, that were parked on the ground and Mrs Khan had strictly directed all the teachers and *sevikas* not to allow the children to come near the car, lest they do some damage. There weren't any playgrounds in the neighbourhood, which meant that boys and girls from the adjacent slums could come in and play on the ground. The people in the slums overlooking the school ground used the ground to throw their garbage from their windows, all of which would land on the hind side of the school. No one complained. No one raised a voice because everything *was* okay.

Work formally began on the Monday of my sixth week of teaching when the school was taken over by a squad of masons and constructors who were renovating the leaking ceilings and cracked floors in the building. The work was initiated by the Corporator, who was under some pressure to show that the municipal funds were being put to public good. Not unsual though, the work began in the middle of the term and without any pre-planning whatsoever as to how the school would operate.

Mrs Khan called me to her office.

"You will have to vacate your classrooms for a few weeks."

At first I thought that I would be shifted to new classroom but when she was not making any sounds to that effect, I curiously asked, "Where do I take my class then?"

She didn't answer.

"We have to figure that out. You know that we don't have enough space for all the students and with so many students, I don't know for now what we can do."

I guessed what she might be thinking of in her mind.

"I cannot ask my children to stay away in the middle of the term," I said. "They are already three grade levels behind and I have just started teaching. If we keep them away for a few weeks, they are going to fall further behind and it would be extremely difficult to pull them up academically when they come back."

"What is the alternative?"

True, there was really no alternative.

That day, many different classrooms were then merged with each other and teachers present were asked to take class as they thought fit among themselves. The fourth and the third graders were put together in one classroom while the second and the first graders were in another. How could we possibly teach two or three different curriculums at the same time?

Added to the agony of teaching was the incessant noise of the hammers and the drilling machines the masons had brought with them. I tried to speak as loudly as I could but nothing worked except to fuel the chances of a turbulent scrimmage breaking out anytime in any of the classrooms. Needless to say, the distractions caused by the masons did conjure iniquities in the minds of the students that broke out on the third day as a civil war between three girls and two boys. In the break time, these girls, all from sixth grade, were making their way through the mess left behind by the masons at the top of the staircase when one of the boys from the Urdu-medium section teased a girl, who was allegedly seeing another guy in the Urdu-medium, and his comrade lifted her skirt up. The victims walked away in silence as the boys kept uttering defiant comments about her, hoping to get a chippy response. Then five minutes later, the girls were back in the corridors, arm-wrestling with the boys. They were joined by ten to twelve other girls from different classrooms. These boys from the Urdu-medium however were so relentlessly stony with their armament of unholy strength that they pulled the girls by their hair and thrashed some of them against the machines. A massive assault followed, in which one boy slashed open a girl's forearm by a blade. The two *sevikas* and I came to the rescue, but got hurt ourselves. A flurry of slangs hit my face accompanied by a gobbet of spit.

The party ceased broke when Mrs Khan came upstairs and nabbed the fomenters. She made them stand in a line on the field outside so that everybody could see them. In this queue, I found that one of my own students, Faisal, was standing. After Mrs Khan finished with them, I heard him muttering as he walked past her, "Some day, I will kill you, bitch."

After a week, I told Mrs Khan that I had decided to isolate my students from the scourge of the sixth grade boys and took my class into the corridor. My decision to do so was well-timed because the masons were now working in the right end of the corridor leaving the left side free from the noises of their machines. My judgement was however not welcomed by the school.

"Why do you have to bother so much about your students," Mrs Khan said. "I think it was better that the classes were combined. If you cannot control so many students, then we can send someone else, but again, there is no urgent need to teach your students at this time. They can easily wait for another two weeks until all the repair work is complete." I was infuriated from inside but kept my calm.

"The students are becoming very disruptive in this environment," I replied politely, "and I think keeping them together is creating more trouble for everybody. Two more weeks is a lot of time. Anyway so many students in the school don't have benches to sit. We don't do anything about it."

"Try if you can but I don't see any use in this at all," she agreed, reluctantly. "But if any parent complains to me, then I won't be able to help you."

I did not expect that I would receive any help from her side and hoped that there would be another group whose help I whole-heartedly sought- that of my own students. That very day, I called them during the break time and explained the situation slowly. I asked them whether they would be comfortable studying in the corridor with me, elaborately explicating all the possible circumstances that may arise out of the new arrangement.

A minute passed with students looking at each other's faces. Then a reply came.

"We have no problems with sitting in the corridor, and we will help you conduct classes without any disturbance." Faisal held the whole class in surprise with his overwhelmingly positive response.

It must have been an augury of the things to come.

FIVE

Of all things that had gone wrong for years at Mahadeo Govind Ranade School, what ached me most was that children in the school were discouraged from asking questions or thinking about what they were taught. The teachers in my school never acknowledged the value of critical thinking in education and hence it had never found itself into practice. Their job seemed only to make parcels of instruction to serve the targets of completing the coursework for every month, whether in reading, writing, science, history, geography, or art.

Sadly the lack of independent thinking had left our children at the mercy of their quotidian habits inculcated through blind imitation of the acts of their teachers. They also liked it that way, perhaps, because exerting a definitive control on the children gave them an inward feeling of gratification. If a student questioned, the teacher thought that he had problem or a disorder of some kind. "The subject matter was there, the text books were there- what *is* there to ask?", said one teacher to me. As I saw it, there was disorder indeed, the kind that results from the mind-crushing load of information dismembered from reality and from thoughtful action.

The first time I had taken a class on drawing, I had asked children to sketch out their house and their immediate neighbourhood. I was surprised when all but one girl drew a house with mountains in the background. I asked several of them and they told me that this was the drawing they knew, so they drew it. I realized that in all the previous years, they had been taught to copy only this one landscape again and again from the board and this monotonous process of copying the drawings from the board had mutilated their power of expression.

When I told the teachers about the problem, a glazed look spread across their visage and in their impatience, the children were, as always, bluntly blamed for the lack of original thinking. The teachers unanimously agreed that *these* children had neither the capacity nor the interest to appreciate, and therefore practice, the intricate details of art. They advised me to not bother so much about such *little* things. Lilting with bafflement, I kept quiet again.

No sin seemed to me more punishable than the slow death of a child's mind. As I went through their work that day, I was so enraged that I felt like razing the whole system of education to the ground.

Quite similar was the situation in more rigid disciplines like Math and English. On the first Math test that I gave my children, the class average came to 16, the top score being 24 out of 100. In English, the average came to 14. This was the way things were since the start of their school lives. In the school that I went to, getting below 75 in maths was always frowned upon. In college, everyone carried high GPAs in their pockets. Here, mediocrity was honoured. To think where we were in our school lives and where these children were dropped my eyes in shame. It was the shame of a nation.

Children in my classroom wanted to tell me only that which they thought would win my approval for that was the way they had been educated. Most of them would not even have the courage to ask me the spelling of a word they did not know. Instead, they preferred to keep their mouths shut and stop working altogether in the fear that I might reproof them. That was where I would miss half of the students from my class. Slowly these students would then begin to cut my classes because they themselves knew that they were falling behind.

The other great impediment to teaching was oblivion. Children had already forgotten things they had learned in previous classes and the eternal fear of books swept from their memories all the lessons that I taught daily. Every day, I would try teaching a lesson in Math or English or a different subject, and the next day over half the children could not tell what had been taught. For the whole of the first month, I taught the same lessons over and over again hoping that children will be able to recollect until I realized that it made no sense to teach something that was simply irrelevant to the way these children had been raised or taught. It was imperative for them to overcome this sheer impoundment of disinterest that years of neglect in school had brought unto them. I realized that learning would never take place if I only taught them how to find answers to questions by bluntly memorizing the rules of grammar and mathematics or exchanging words.

It was only after many initial frustrations that I found a panacea. I decided to introduce something that they hadn't experienced or heard before. I wanted to convince and convert them by observation, wonder, supposition, dream, doubt, action, conflict, ambition, participation and regret.

They did not like the battered hand-me-down textbooks that had been given to them by the school and I did not like them either. It was boring, lifeless and unexciting and many had already torn apart their schoolbooks in defiance and protest. Those that had managed to remain intact were never opened.

I had made up my mind. I would not teach the books that had been handed out to children year after year. I wanted my children to explore the richness of classics and poetry, to learn about nature's gifts, about the rich diversity of life and to appreciate freedom and expression. After about a month of frivolous ransacking of the shelves of half a dozen bookshops, I ultimately found the book that been one of my favourite reading materials as a child. Jules Verne's "Twenty Thousand Leagues under the Sea".

While the idea sounded great, there were obvious challenges in teaching such a difficult novel to children who have only begun to write and read with ease. Many of the words in the book would be difficult for them to even pronounce correctly and there were many in my class who were not yet ready for such a book. So, I kept putting my idea away for weeks and instead focussed on building the phonetic strength of my children.

The thrill of teaching Jules Verne however had gripped me like a boa constrictor and the first story telling class began in October. We were in the hall room that day, all alone. The children sat in half-circular fashion around a chair which I secured from another classroom. I had purchased copies of the novel for all the children and they had their books opened before them. I gave them a good ten minutes to go through the book and the few illustrations it contained. Then, in a voice trickling with fear and adventure, I read out the first line, "The Year 1866 was signalized by a remarkable incident…."

The lesson went on for an hour. They rolled their eyes at their story books, ran through the pages across their thumbs or simply stared at me with irresistibly enamoured eyes, gripped and mesmerized by each sentence that I explained to them. One of the boys in front laid down his whole body on the floor, slowly, part by part, without even knowing that he was clad from chest to feet in dust.

Captain Nemo had come as an envoy from the fairer courts of life to touch my children with wonder and ecstasy. Although Twenty Thousand Leagues was the only novel I was able to teach in the year, its verdant prose had charmed them to the rising din of discovery. Like the enigmatic Nemo himself, children were travelling into the far reaches of new seas of mystery that lay before them. Every Wednesday, we read a chapter of the book. Slowly and steadily, the Nautilus of their dreams explored the hidden treasures of endless worlds. After every class, children flooded me with questions and guesses about what would happen in the end. They were impatient but they never dared to turn the page to the last chapter. Not even secretly.

From that time on, my children were passionately submerged in their own intellectual discoveries. There was absolutely nothing that they could not grasp; nothing seemed out of their cognitive limits. They wanted to experiment with everything and it seemed that suddenly our educational studio had turned into a hive of activity. We wrote, we sang, we acted, we recited poems and read stories.

While so much had never taken place in the years gone by, Mrs Khan kept complaining that I was not following the academic curriculum set by the *Education Board*. She was annoyed and surprised that I was trying all sorts of insanities in my classroom that seemed to have no importance or meaning at all. The other teachers soon began to share her discomfort. Yet these apparently insane things seemed to fit so easily into what my children were familiar with that I decided not to say much. I only held my peace and tried to work with what I planned every day, only reassuring myself that everything will soon fall in place.

After about four months of teaching, the first terminal examination was conducted. It turned out to be a personal test for me as well given that I had only managed to invite the discontentment of Mrs Khan and the other teachers. The average score in our classroom had kissed an all-time high of 67 in English and 60 in Mathematics while children in the other classrooms had managed to secure barely a third of what we got. Their teachers later on made them pass by manipulating their scores. In my class also, there were a dozen who cared so less about passing or failing that they had submitted blank answer scripts but the class on the whole had progressed to unprecedented levels.

Our performance was extraordinary by all means and it bought me appreciation from Mrs Khan. Although I did not vie for her adulation, it still felt good that the teachers were now talking about me. Inwardly however, I knew I had not done anything miraculous at all. As a matter of fact, I had deliberately tried to keep most of my lessons as simple and unscholarly as possible. During the weeks when I was struggling to maintain discipline and peace in my classroom, I had only succeeded in teaching very little, mostly about the things that I knew best and things that I appreciated, which included some ideas of geometry, a few facts and physical laws, painting, stories about men, nature and a few short poems. I knew very well then how naïve and unmindful and even clumsy I was when it came to matters of pedagogy and how in my earnest attempts to hide my inexperience I often ended up making a travesty of my idiocy and lack of sophistication.

However, the saving grace was that by now I knew each child's learning styles and the way they preferred to learn- often through drawings, writings, graphs, poetry or music and this helped to keep my focus on their individual responses rather than on the mere subject matter of my lessons. But somewhere in my efforts to bring back the harmony which had been lost long ago in my classroom, I had inadvertently dared into the unknown and introduced my children to a world where knowledge is free, where they could find the truth about themselves and liberate themselves from the prison of miseducation. There was no fear in them but sympathy, love and the greatness of the good. Into that world, I believed my children had woken up with a moral wisdom as ripe as a fruit in season. Like life itself, growing in a curtilage of living aspiration.

SIX

The aromas of success come to different people in different corsages. I had been basking in glory of the remarkable achievements and the victories of the first term for it was the first trophy I had raised after a long and relentless struggle and I wanted to herald to the parents of my students the progress they had made in just half a year.

For months I had tried to picture in my mind how this day would be and what I would like to say to the parents. I wanted to surprise them, I wanted to magnetize them, I wanted to see a gleam of satisfaction illuminating their faces when I tell them that the inhibitions of the bygone years no longer existed, that they would not be stultified by the incompetence of those who were in responsible for their education and that from here on there would always be something new to look forward to.

I had been preparing and rehearsing my speeches ever since the date was announced, working very hard to perfect my intonation and delivery at every point. I wanted my presentation to be terse but enlightening at the same time. I knew that there were many parents who had mounting grievances about the school's worsening facilities and the declining quality of education that it proffered. Nevertheless, this was the first time I was going to meet them all together and talk about their children, their ambitions and their dreams. There was so much I had already known about my children and yet I had the feeling that I knew almost nothing about them. I wanted the parents to fill the gaps, to learn from them every minute detail about my children that I could not perceive in class.

But while all this excitement was spouting out of me at terrific speed, Mrs Khan did her best to curb my interest. She told me that although she made arrangements for the parents every term, it was always a futile exercise for hardly any of the parents bothered to turn up. "You should observe the other teachers. None of them are putting in half the efforts that you are. They are all going to keep it short. We have all known these parents for so many years now. Do you think they understand a thing about education that they are going to come asking you how their children are doing in class? These poor parents are *like* that- they don't care about it. That's how it has always been."

Thinking she was being overly pessimistic and unreasonable, I decided to shrug off her remarks.

"This time will be different," I replied politely.

"We shall see then how things go," she replied with a close-lipped smile.

The meeting was scheduled on a Thursday at four in the afternoon. That day, there was no school and parents were supposed to accompany their children to collect the reports from the teachers. Being very fastidious about this auspicious occasion, I had designed in advance a special invitation card which contained hand-written notes for each of the sixty five families that filled my class. I had searched and found out the names of the parents from the registers kept in the school. I decked up my classroom and carefully managed to fit about forty odd chairs. Given how small our classroom was, all this had taken nearly two hours.

My enthusiasm was welling over the rim as I waited impatiently at the corner of the door for the students to come accompanying their parents. I looked at my watch. Four fifteen, it said. There were a few mothers who came in and out of the other classrooms but none came within even twenty yards of our room.

Four forty five. My restlessness was growing. I started walking back and forth along the length of the corridor. I passed the classroom of the fifth standard. There was no one in there. The fourth standard classroom had two parents waiting at the door, but there was no teacher inside. The parents probably did not know that till now, this class did not have a teacher.

As I walked ahead, I saw a woman standing at the opening of the staircase. She was looking this way and that, confused which way to go. I thought she was looking for my classroom. I rushed to her in quick steps.

"Are you looking for seventh standard classroom?" I asked.

"No, my son is in the third standard. Can you show me which room is it?" I obliged politely.

I looked at my watch again. Five fifteen. The time now told me that no one would come for the reports. The avidity with which my day began was now downed in dejection. It was pointless to wait any longer. I started putting the progress cards I had written for my children into my bag and turned to leave. Just then I stumbled against a middle-aged woman who had come in through the door and stood right behind me. She had been standing so quietly at my back that I had no hint of her presence. Collecting myself, I tried to put up a wide smile and welcomed her as an empty gesture but she turned her face away in disregard.

We sat face to face. She was wearing an old sari, whose colour had faded to a faint reddish hue, one end of which was tied to her waist. She looked at me with a pair of cold inexpressive eyes and curled eyebrows.

A few minutes passed. I was hoping she would begin but her diffidence seemed to possess her wholly. I saw that she was looking around the room and decided to give her some more time, while I pretended to be busily engaged in searching through my papers for the report of her child.

"You are….?" I asked.

"Gayatri's report," she answered.

I recognized her in an instant. Gayatri was famous in the school, for she lived in a nearby Vishnu temple, where her father was a priest.

Being possessed with a quick and penetrating intelligence and quite a self-starter for a girl of her age, Gayatri had earned the heartfelt affection at the hands of the teachers. She was elegant to her fingertips in the way she preened- she would come every day with impeccable tidiness, her uniform washed and ironed, her shoes polished, her hair well-knit, her books covered with brown-paper. These things were quite insignificant to me given that none of my other students could afford to be so exhibitionist, yet somehow her outward elements of grace always made

Gayatri more conspicuous than the other children in the classroom.

Gayatri was possessed by an all-encompassing dream of going to college. Very few in her neighbourhood had leaped over the boundary wall of primary and upper primary school. Going to college would naturally make her intellectually more superior than the rest of the people in the neighbourhood. However in these neighbourhoods college was not seen as an impossible thing to achieve academically; for them, the opportunity cost of allowing their children to study until college was enormously high.

"One must have a lot of money to go to college," Gayatri had told me. "My parents do not have enough to keep me in school for that long. But once I reach class eight, I would start providing tuition to the other children in the neighbourhood. There are no good tuition teachers in our neighbourhood. Those that are there have passed only class six or seven. All the English they know ends at nursery rhymes. They can't teach English-medium children properly. I would make a lot of money from it and that money will help me. I would be able to buy more books to study."

As a teacher, I did my best to add fuel to the flaming alter of her ambitions, explaining to her the entire process of matriculating to a college, the concept of an Honours course and the system of grading followed in most colleges in our country. She listened patiently with wide-eyed eagerness, asking various questions and situations to clarify.

I had, in my zest to encourage her further, collected a list of scholarships made available by the Government and some NGOs to disadvantaged girls who wanted to continue with their studies. "I would work ten times harder than everyone else," she said, "to get those scholarships. My parents then would not have to bear the trouble of supporting my education."

Gayatri had acquired the highest scores in my class in all the tests and considering the neighbourhood she came from and the peers she was growing up with, I thought it was truly a terrific thing to achieve. Seeing her results, I had guessed that she had a fairly good chance at cracking the Maharashtra talent scholarship for the seventh standard. No one from the school had cracked the test in the last ten years. The teachers themselves did not believe that it was possible for any child from this school to be able to qualify. However, the optimist in me saw things otherwise and I was contemplating about how to prepare her for the qualifying test. If she could win it, she would be paid a hundred rupees every month as long as she continued with her education. That was a lot of money for her. Yet when I explained to her mother about my hopes of seeing her through the scholarship, her mother threw a cursive glance at the report card and turned it upside down on the table and glanced at me in a way that immediately told me that she was hardly interested in her accomplishments. She looked at me with a glance that was at the same time suspicious, untrusting and calculating.

Constantly grappling with her unaccommodating nature, I finally asked her quizzically to elicit if she had any concerns, "Do you have anything to say?"

She thought for a while and then spoke. "Gayatri says that you don't make her sit in the first row. In her previous classes, she always sat in the first row. The teachers thought she was bright. *Kai aaiku yennar o yevhadya lamb?* (How can a child hear from so far?) She says you make all those other boys and girls who have no business coming to school sit in the first rows. You don't need to pay attention to them. There come to school for food and make this place dirty. What else! My child is bright and smart; she needs the teacher's attention. If you don't separate her from the lot, then she will also become like them. I don't want that to happen."

I had not imagined that anyone would have a problem in the way children sat in my class, and that such little things would make parents and children worry. I tried explaining to her but saw that she was not contented for she shook her head from right to left in denial. She kept on arguing that it was not okay to let Gayatri mix freely with everyone else in the classroom.

"Sir, you are new to this school. Am I right?" she asked me.

I was a little surprised. I politely nodded.

"Then let me tell you something sir. You don't know how these neighbourhoods are. You are new here. If you knew the place well enough, you would have been less carefree and more cautious." Like a cat in a gutter, I stared at her, still and motionless. She continued in the same tone, " We have been living here for forty five years. In our times, we Brahmins were the only people in the neighbourhood. But then people of all sorts started to come in here. First there were few. They did not even have places to stay. They stayed in houses made of bamboo and plastic. Some of them used to spend nights sleeping on the staircases of our buildings. They made more and more money whereas back in the villages they would have to go and work in the fields.

"Gradually, they got their entire families up here and encouraged other people from their villages to come and find work here. They started encroaching into every open ground and building and converted them into slums." As she spoke, I stared outside the window, with the growing sadness of a tree with no leaves. The neighborhood showed its teeth, filling me with utter abjection and despair once again.

"Then crimes started happening. People started ruling over us and meeting out punishments. That was when the Brahmins decided to move out of this neighbourhood. Over the last ten years, we saw all the Brahmins changing their areas and moving to better areas like Narayan Peth and Sadashiv Peth because there aren't any low-caste or Muslim families out there. They have rebuilt those areas and made sure that only they are living there. There are very schools too. All the troubles are in this godforsaken side where we are stuck forever because we are poor. Why would I want to live in a neighbourhood where I am surrounded by these people? They are not that bad but we don't fit with them in any way. We cannot eat with them, we cannot sit with them because we do not choose to live in way they choose to live."

I stared at her, cold in surprise. Her tone became thick with disdain and self-rejection.

"When these Muslim and low-castes families started putting their children in school, we were alarmed. This school was our object of pride. If you look at the records of the school some fifteen years back, it was one of the best public schools in the city. Look at the condition now. And why would anyone waste his time in teaching poor people? They know education doesn't happen in a slum. Never.

"The Brahmins have all withdrawn their children out of fear of co-mingling with these people. We are the only Brahmin family, still left out here. Now they send them to private schools, which they all say, have better environment. If we had money, we would have never kept our girl in such a school in this neighbourhood. How can you feel safe here?"

She stopped and exhaled. She greatly suffered in her incapacity to accept that her child would have to experience the misfortune of studying in a school that was open to *everyone* in the neighbourhood, that the fate of her education was inextricably knotted to the fate of an abandoned school that was struggling to support an abandoned neighbourhood.

It could be true that as the neighbourhood had altered in shape and spirit, the school also had transformed itself from a favourable seat of learning into a factory for producing a litany of failures year after year and its ruination had closely followed the pattern of economic change brought about when many more deeply disadvantaged families began to fill into the gaps in this place.

A couple of private schools had quickly sprouted like mushrooms which, although did not guarantee a better quality of learning standards, charged tuition fees well above the economic limits of these poor families. The tuition fee was perhaps a symbol of class and prestige, but not an indicator of good education. The schools also controlled in many other subtle discretionary ways who they admitted every year, how many in a class were from minorities sections, culturally and religiously.

"But it's not just a matter of money, you know," Gayatri's mother continued in her lugubrious way. "It's just not an honourable way to live. These schools are not for our children. Our children cannot sit in the same room with these people. We never let her go outside the house for the whole day. It is only during school that she is away. I know for a fact that Gayatri is learning all kinds of filthiness here. She is learning all their language and their slangs. You cannot see it because you don't know what it is to live in a neighbourhood like ours. I don't blame you for that.

"All our people ask us to take her out of school and to keep her at home instead. We get humiliated by them all the time. We are always in constant fears. My Gayatri is only 11 years old. Look at the other boys and girls- some of them are already 15 or 16 years of age. If something happens to my daughter tomorrow, can we show our faces to anyone? We suffer because the neighbourhood suffers. But what other option do we have? We have often thought of going back to our village, but we cannot anymore."

She lifted the hanging edge of her sari that was folded at her waist and rubbed the disappointment that had blackened her face. It was the disappointment of witnessing the erosion of one's values and finding one's innermost beliefs under threat. We sat quietly for some time. I kept looking at her while her eyes were fixed to the ground. I felt sorry for her but did not know of anything that I could say to appease her for now.

That was how perhaps every parent here felt. Coming to school perhaps reminded them of their own painful recollections of the many disappointments and humiliations that stood in the way of their education, of their differences, the divisions and the inhibitions that together brought about their failures. Perhaps it evoked in them a deep insecurity about themselves and the children. Perhaps that was the reason why they distrusted us and preferred not to come to school to talk about children.

Gayatri's mother had left me in a strange state of uneasiness with shattering feelings about my apparent success. Just when I was beginning to think that my children were going to turn the tables, I was rattled by the irreconcilable conflicts and suspicions they were growing up with. That thought pierced me like a shaft, clear and cold.

I reclined into a state of deep delirium and sighed as I stared blankly at the long lines of empty chairs which had not been filled up by my guests. The more I pondered over their differences, the more I swirled into perplexity and heartbrokenness. I had never before considered it possible that these narrow invisible walls would tear the ever-widening minds of my children. Maybe, I did not understand these doctrines of doubt and divisions well enough. As a teacher, I tried to look upon each of my children with equal dignity and with the all the tenderness of my heart; it did not matter to me whether one was Hindu and the other was Muslim, whether he was low-caste or Brahmin. I forgave them for those little differences. But for the people in these neighbourhoods, these imbecilities perhaps came for a higher price than a good education.

Maybe Gayatri's mother was right- it depended on what people chose for them. Maybe it was better to live under the shadow of a crushing lie that education would get them to a better place someday. Maybe it made more sense to send children to a school than to drop them off a kerbstone where the realities were unmistakably worse. Maybe one had to choose which side one wanted to be. That way one could avoid falling off the margins of an unremitting city where there was no place for them. Maybe that gave them the hope to live in a world where reason faded into the air like water evaporating from a glass left open in the summer heat. Those were the pacts they made with themselves. Those were the choices they had picked.

SEVEN

By the first three months of my teaching, I had come to accept that I was the only stable entity in the universe of chaos that surrounded our school and no matter how hard I tried to install rules and consequences, the lawlessness continued to meander its way into my bay. Being an old hat, I had originally set up five common rules to bring some order in my class, these being, *raise your hands before you speak, do not fight with others, remain seated during the class, be gentle and polite* and *finish your work every day,* but frankly I don't remember even one of them being ever observed by the children. On some days, the control I had over my class was completely illusory in the face of all the catcalls hurtled in my honour and I think I had been utterly foolish to assume that children had not been taught these rules before; in fact, they knew something more, how to get around and shoot past rules. Instead of accepting my rules, the students had enacted their own unwritten codes of defiance. Rules and Defiance thus played a ceaseless cat and mouse race and with every day ending in near self-defeat, I would recline with fatigue in the school's office with a broken soul and often an injured arm. There I sat paralyzed for hours and tried to stitch the worn-out threads of my tolerance. I knew how helpless and worried I looked, not because I had just witnessed a day being burned down like a splith of light but because I would have to reeve through the same ring of fire on the next day as well.

However, there was one thing that had quietly begun to reverse the tides in my classroom. It was the letter writing class on Saturday. This day was the perfect setting for this class because the most notorious children deliberately cut school on this day. Yet for a teacher trying to tame sixty six children and often many more, it was one of those rare days that I held dear. On these afternoons, my children weaved the wool of their experiences through letters written in their own hands and read them aloud to their audience.

In the months preceding my arrival at Mahadeo Govind Ranade School, when I had been negotiating and renegotiating in my mind the endless ways in which I wanted to help children appreciate the fullness of the English language, this format of writing exercise had prod me more than once for it was among the few elements of learning that I had a special liking for in my own school days. For me, it was fascinating to see how far my thoughts could travel.

In the first two months of my time as a teacher, I had laboriously drilled into my students dozens of new words, phrases and structures to construct sentences, because without these everything would be illegible to them. Children had picked up very fast and learned to write bits and pieces of English correctly. Like always, it had taken me a while to get over my doubts that children would not be able to write well or end up simply abusing or deriding others.

What happened however was completely unanticipated and truly remarkable.

Time permitted only three students to speak on one afternoon, which gave children the freedom to draft their letters for several weeks until they felt they were ready. In the dullness of these afternoons, I would retreat to the middle of the room and forcefully squeeze myself into a little space, often by folding up my arms and legs, among the hordes of faces that piled up around me.

One of these letters was written by Salman, a quiet, disconcerted-looking boy who had spent several years of his childhood in a remote village in Aurangabad. He shared with the entire class the demises of almost three quarters of his kinsmen in droughts. His was a story of struggling to adjust to the ways of a haggard and hungry life upon the platforms of the city's railway station. There they lived for a few years until they were pushed out by the government onto a slum behind the last platform. Here in their urban exile, they put their shaky hands to reconstruct the threads of life once again.

Through tough alleys Salman had learned to fight his own battles, ever since he was four years of age. Salman had unconditionally made friends with hunger because as a child, he had been told to believe that hunger would never go away. It was the first of many pre-conditions to their survival. The other one was the fear of the police. He wrote how often the police would come looking for his brothers and often his friends, who were accused of petty thefts of coal and kerosene to make up for the lack of electricity and gas. That need was so acute that no one would open their mouths when the policemen enquired them. Sometimes,

they would slap Salman for lying or hit him with their stick
but he said, "It was okay." He felt like a hero in his slum
whenever he did not bend. At this juncture, Salman also
confessed in his letter that he was the person who had picked
my wallet from my trousers in the first week of school.

Salman's father had died in the drought and his mother
who was half-dead from periodic attacks of typhoid and
malaria earned to see him go to school. She said to him, "If
you go to school, the *policewallas* will not beat you." While
that was one reason, the other reason Salman thought why
his mother forced him every day to go to school was rooted
in her deep sense of pride for her son. It was a matter of
prestige in their slum to have a son who went to school.
She went about concocting cock-and-bull stories about how
intelligent her son is and how his teachers praised him all the
time. She told the slum dwellers that one day when he passes
out of school, he will get a job in one of the tall offices that
could be seen against the city's expanding skyline from the
roof of their hut. But for Salman, it was nothing more than
her empty vanity. For Salman, school was merely one of
those sorting systems built to make him stupid and foolish.
Since the day he came to school, he had known what a boy
of his provenance really could be and he knew it better than
his mother.

Salman stopped halfway for breath, so I thought. His
face, set to a grim expression, looked darkened with the
connate pain from wounds that had not been healed for
a long time. But he held the letter in his hand and only
stared. A few minutes passed, followed by a few more. He
lapsed deeper into silence and closed his eyelids as if he
suffered a sudden spasm of despair and then turning away,

he crumpled the paper inside his meaty grip as if it meant nothing to him. When the day was finally over, I had happened to pick up the missive of his life, stamped by the dirt under the children's shoes, from the corner of the room.

Salman had been wrestling with the question of why he should come to school at all because for years he had been sitting in the classrooms, sometimes repeatedly, where nothing interesting was going on. There was always so much more he could do to help his family tie the split ends of their circumstances. He often cut school and went and sat outside a motor-garage behind the school. The owner of that place was quick to notice him and asked him if he would work. The first time he got ten rupees paid in coins of ones and twos, he felt like a big man because his pocket felt heavy and made sounds when he walked back home. No one in the neighbourhood believed that he had made it out of hard work. They thought he had stolen it.

When he was in the fourth standard, his mother was taken down by flu which had rung red alarms across the city. The school had been shut down for months. During that time, Salman avoided school and worked in the garage almost five hours every day and to a certain degree he became an expert, in repairing wipers, brake shoes and suspensions and painting motor-vehicles. He made thirty rupees there for a day's work.

While many of the boys were candid about their experiences and wrote on a variety of subjects, the girls were not. I understood the difficulty. It was indeed uncomfortable to talk to a room full of teenage boys and a male teacher. That inhibition forced them to quietly put their letters onto the shelves and I worried that they would never trust me enough to read their letters. It changed when a girl stood up one day and said, "I want to read my letter today."

Noor was a fifteen-year old girl, with a face as wrinkled as an old pair of trousers and with scrolls of golden hair felted up like the ends of carpet and pushed inside her burqa. I had never thought that she would have any interest in drafting a letter, because it was evident that she came to school for all reasons other than studying. She was one of those girls who could never accept authority at face value. If she was disturbed or offended she would settle matters with the power of her fists. Clouded by some inscrutable feeling of insecurity, she would pick fights on the slightest insults. It was for the same reason that many boys, and even girls, tried to prey on her by intentionally bullying and hectoring her. I would hear her say, "*Tu tameez se bat kar*" and the very next moment, she would be goggling at them with indignation and firing a torrent of invectives, ultimately breaking the class into a kerfuffle. Yet being a girl, she was always losing her fights against the boys; she was like a drowning person, biting her opponents, throwing herself on the floor, kicking and flailing, and reaching out for anything near her hands-pencil boxes, compasses, duster, sandals- that might save her. But she would still fight till the end in a desperate struggle. I did not understand why.

Noor lived in the slums of Lohiyanagar. Her father was an infamous personality in the neighbourhood and also in our school for almost every child and teacher knew about him. He had mated with four women in their slum alone and had several children born of those women. Some even suspected that he had relations with several more women in the neighbouring slums. He had disappeared from their lives many years ago and the family was taken care of by Azhar, her half-brother.

Noor wrote her a letter where she described in vivid details how Azhar who was ten years older, had forced her into several intercourses with his group of friends. Sometimes several of them assaulted her at the same time while sometimes her brother needed her to satisfy his own retardant wishes. She wrote she felt she was dead every time they plundered her. Despite knowing everything, her mother had been keeping her mouth shut. "You are a girl," she read out her mother's words. "You cannot tell no to your brother. This is your world." She wrote that she believed her mother also had been forced to go to bed with him. She did not feel sorry for her though. She did not hate her brother though. She hated herself more. For the whole world seemed to her like a grotesque chimaera of imagination battering her against the obstacles of denial and hatred.

It blew me out of my world to believe these words were coming out from the girl whose hands and fingernails did all the talking. Everyone knew how igneous this girl was and it seemed impossible that she had never protested against the crimes done to her. But on this day, Noor was someone else, someone we did not know, limpid and tranquil, like the silence that reposed in the room. It felt as if the strength that she always showed in her fights was ebbing away. That indeed she lost her predominant characteristic- confidence. In the silent lines of her lips and between the lashes of her eyes, there was now a voice of a plain acceptance of her status, like the goat raised only to be immolated on the day of festival. This, she wrote, was the rule of her world. This was the rule she could not afford to break.

A part of me has often wondered why she had no respect for the rules of the class, why she was the one who tore those paper cuttings apart every time I had them pasted on the door. It perhaps stemmed from her sneering unbelief in the orders of the world that she fiercely wanted to dismantle all the rules that she saw before her.

Her face was aflame and scalding water trembled on the side of her nose, its vacant holes had swollen with shame, agony and fear and her throat that was clear and resolute at the start had begun to judder through the depths of her truth.

She withdrew herself slowly like a livid quivering mass. At one time, I had stood up nervously, fearing that the gangsters of my class could throw a merciless joke at her anytime and I would have to step in and cover her. But gravity kept them sitting motionlessly through her horrors. Some were looking with fixed eyes at the floor, probably contemplating, while some kept their eyes shut and covered their faces throughout her narrative. Others stared outside the window without bating their eyelids.

Perhaps they were enwrapped in their own harrowing memories. Perhaps they were realizing that they were united by interests that were more common than the difference that comes from being a girl over a boy or the difference that comes from stealing an extra rupee from the pockets of their classmates. Perhaps there was no difference at all between those feelings in an unchanging world.

Many of these letters that I still possess were gibberish and lacked the sophistication, variety and artistry of a literary composition; many were written in direct rebellion against the phonetic and grammatical principles of the English language that attempting to read these letters on my own became an almost impossible feat. To me, the children's ways of living strikingly matched the children's way of writing. It was only a manifestation of the chaos that lived inside them, the chaos they had no control over. Like the heaps of garbage that accumulated around their slums, their handwritings were dirty, illegible and their words herded like the overcrowding of their slums. There would be no full-stops, commas and other punctuation marks which in point of fact were also forever missing in their lives. Because the commas and colons always seemed to be disappearing from their lives. Because they themselves did not know where their stories ended.

These were not careless mistakes. Rather they were matters of choice. Children could never guess what the right punctuation would be, because they did not know what it took to make a right choice, because every choice they had ever made in their lives had turned out wrong.

I had never heard such letters before. For they were real letters, letters that threw light into the thick layers of turpitude that the world had shoved into their daily drama of their lives. Many of the letters talked of dreams that perhaps would never materialize, expectations that were never met and of those countless disappointments. They were real letters that turned over the pages of pain and grief, of doubt and disbelief, of shame and disgrace, of disillusion and failure confined through perpetuity. A million thoughts jostled for space in our small room and arguments and dilemmas queued up.

And yet in these letters, I had discovered a tremendous fact of human experience: that behind the shades of animosity and pugilism, my children were endowed with courage, dedication and heroism that was beyond ordinary human love. They had the courage to defend their dignity, even if it meant to spill blood from their bodies and hate another child with infernal intensity. They held the conviction to open their hearts and accept the other's place in their lives by the same reasons that they accepted the inevitability about themselves. It was fearless to have a faith that someday things will change when there was actually none. No book, no teacher and no school had taught them that courage, only life had.

It would not be enough to say in words but I discovered at that moment that my children possessed a rather savage will inside them, the will to fight, just to live. It is not something ordinary and innate that I have come across before. Most of us adults may often give up thinking that there is no point or lose hope quite easily. But there are some that never give up. They fight and fight and fight. And still fight, bravely, regardless of the gains or pains. And in that sense, all my children were real heroes in their lives who were reluctant to accept that their lives were meaningless, that their education was over. With all the strength in their mind, they wanted to deny the reality of how ugly and poor they were, to deny that hope was a privilege they couldn't afford.

The stories buried in their letters had made me feel deep pain for the first time in all my years of growing up. As if the edge of disbelief was corrugated. Like a piece of metal turned up by a milling machine. Their experiences were far too great to overcome; it had raised the stakes of the ephemeral nature of their survival to a frightening degree. For days, I felt blunted by the absolute insensitiveness and wickedness lurking in the fabric of their world. Where survival itself was a great gift, a fortune not to be spared, it was extraordinary how these little hapless souls held themselves up through one tragedy after another. I saw the strength of the human spirit, its heroism, its faith and its humanity.

As a teacher, I have often on many days been cast under the doubt, thinking over and again that I should give up. Maybe I would have, but a number of voices sounded in my heart that said that I will not let this happen to my children. I will help them beat the odds, no matter what the chances of success are. I will summon all the strength of my body and all the obduracy of my mind, but I will not let injustice prevail. Those voices had made the teacher in me much stronger than before. I could now absorb reality with greater fortitude and endurance. Misery, death and hope did not anymore affect me as much as it did before. Like my children, I had learned to move forward and fight for a better tomorrow. My respect and the love for my children doubled and it got me much closer to them. The natural barrier between a student and a teacher had dissolved. In seeking the inner secrets that lay within them, the world of my children now suddenly belonged to me. New spaces had opened up and new relationships sprouted in those spaces like buds of flowers embracing the first rays of sunlight. It was as if I had known them for a lifetime. I was a brother to one who had lost a brother, a friend to one who did not have any, a father to one who did not know who his real father was.

In the many roles I played, I talked extensively with my students about life and living. I tried to understand their hopes, their wishes and their interpretations of themselves in the light of others. I pitied the child who had been looking forever for a place to stuff his pity and laughed with the child who could make a joke out of everyone and mimic the voices of teachers. We talked about the power of our will to love and care despite the implacable odds that life throws at us. We learned to share each other's grief and to draw the strength to hold ourselves together. Nearly every day, for hours into the afternoon when school was over, I had sat on the staircase and quietly heard girls like Noor and boys like Salman. They were not alone anymore.

Being miserable was so common in the everyday life of these children that no one really paid any attention to it. To the children however, it was great to have somebody who they could tell everything to. They were secure in knowing that I was a part of their life. This synthesis with children led me to be reborn in new knowledge and new action. I learned to put wisdom together with innocence, strength with flexibility and trust with discernment. When I walked into the classrooms, I could feel the radiant hues kindle upon my students- their faces appeared brighter and their expression only more brilliant. Laughter and mirth became an almost inseparable part of daily routine during our classes where, in the months before, it was didn't exist at all. Lunch time was no longer a battle for me to try and prevent my students from violence. My students now shared their lunch-time with me and although the break was only forty odd minutes long, we seemed to drift away in timeless conversations about each other's lives and families. And of course, dreams that were wrought in gold. Perhaps they found some ray of strength in knowing that I could stay beside them through their lives and encourage them to dream. I tried not to disappoint them.

They believed everything I told them, without even questioning if it was real or not, and then they wanted to hear more about me. We could not stop saying and listening to each other. My children had begun to take pride in the fact that they had a teacher who cared for them and made it a point to show to the rest of the school that they were different. Children from other classrooms began coming to me asking if they could join my art class or poetry class. Personally, I was now quite contented in just having them around me, while at the time when I began teaching I was terrified and nearly at war with them. I began to like the things that interested them not because I was interested in those things but simply because those things excited them. Whenever something wonderful happened in their lives, they couldn't hold their excitement to tell me about it. The very next morning the first thing they would do is come up to me and tell me what happened. When I made mistakes, they came and told me that they did not like it. When I cried, they cried with me. When I made a show of foolishness in the classroom and laughed at myself, they laughed with me. After Akhilesh in my class lost his father who was hit by a train, I went to the funeral. We walked back to his house and all along the way, he had held my hand tightly in his. Two months later when he came back to my class, I knew he was fighting dire circumstances. So the first thing I did was to go up to him and ask him how he was feeling. "When you talk to me," he replied, "life seems so different, so easy. The problems of life do not feel so important anymore. I feel happier. I feel good." I was a witness to that great propensity for goodness. That day, I had realized what teaching was really all about- a set of values deeply intertwined into the garment of life and not a series of chapters bound in the hard covers of books.

EIGHT

Fahd was one of those boys whose zest for play never ceased to amaze me. He always seemed like he was in a hurry. Not that he dashed around in the class or the corridors, but his mind appeared to move very fast, much like a yo-yo. Sadly, being poor he did not have enough toys or games to spend his time. He had no chess boards, puzzles, scrabbles or remote-controlled cars, not even a football of his own. It did not matter much though because the genius in Fahd marveled at inventing his own toys. His hands had been designed with the finesse and sharpness of a shaping machine to carve out his needs right from a tender age. Like a stone-age man, he made most of his toys out of objects lying around his house- bricks, flints, pieces of wood, paper, plastic, or the sole of his school shoes, when he began to feel the road under his feet; all that rich people would throw away as waste somehow circulated their way into the creative and agile hands of Fahd.

Uncomplicated in design and simplistic in style, he began with paper toys like boats and fans. Then he mastered the simple paper rocket. But his first major toy comprised of a piece of wheel that he had picked up from the neighbourhood's trash; he had then searched more and found three more pieces of wheel of similar size and weight. Then with a plank and a rope, he had made his skate board. He showed off his skate board with great pride. It was the object of envy for all the other boys in school. With a big heart, he often gave them his skate board to ride.

The power to create something new out of mere nothings is often so empowering that it sweeps the mind of all other thoughts. For Fahd, it was enmeshed in his blood like an inexpugnable drug. All that he saw with his wide-eyes he made with his hands. He made, again by nibbling the trash and refuse of the neighbourhood, every car that he saw pass by the main avenues of the city. A car shaped like a Mercedes Benz. Another one shaped like a BMW. They were operated by hand. Then he constructed by chiselling out from a stone small deities and demons- Ganesh and Ravan. Being a Muslim had got him considerable embarrassment for making these idols. He had them buried under the soil. Later on, he built a flying helicopter using only light pieces cut out from a bamboo stem and a small electronic motor. This stock of toys must have been larger than that of all the slum children put together. It had yoyos, kites, hoops, spinning tops, skipping ropes, taws and marbles and bows and arrows. For me, though, Fahd was more than a teacher. He showed me how to always remain busy with something.

Fahd was wrapped in another gripping fascination: pigeons. He absolutely loved them but his mother kept complaining to me, asking me to help him get rid of this. Every day, after he came back from school, his mother would force him to sleep. He would however pretend that he was sleeping and when his mother dozed off, he slipped out of the room and went to the roof of their hut. He then spent the whole afternoon jumping barefooted from one roof to another to catch his pigeons.

One afternoon after school, he pulled my hand upto his hut to see how he caught his prey. I had no option. We sat together on the roof and built the trap. A novice in this matter, I only followed his orders. He got ropes and long silk threads, stolen from his mother's basket, and wound them together. The other end of the thread was tied into a loop, so small and thin that it was invisible to the naked eye. The trap was completed when he strew *dana* on the roof but only around the loop to attract the pigeons. Once the pigeon eats the grains, it will have to step into the loop. He will then pull the loop and tie it to pigeon's leg. The mastery of such a trap required great instincts. Fahd had it in him. The little man had earned his reputation for setting traps as early as the age of six. The neighbours often called him to set traps for rats and other rodents that came inside their houses in search of grains. He had never been defeated.

After the hook was ready, we hid under a thick brown blanket and upon it we put a sheet of tin. We remained covered in the darkness behind a small tank. Fahd was holding the end of the rope in his hand waiting for the bird to fall into the loop. He waited for his raven. His heart beat had become slower and his breathing also seemed to have stopped. I could not feel him lying right beside me.

A flock of pigeons came down to the roof flapping their wings in excitement. They looked here and there, inspecting the palace for the presence of snares. Some flew up and again came down. They chatted with each other and took their decision: they would eat the grains today. One of the birds lowered their beaks, one at a time and picked up the pieces. Then another one followed and then the rest.

The birds moved around by tiptoeing all over the place and shared their food. Slowly, more than a dozen pigeons had congregated on the roof and I lost track of where the loop was. The hunter beside me however had not. Like a shark, cold and focussed. Suddenly he raised his index finger and thumb in a queer fashion and I saw a white-grey pigeon fall headfirst on the roof. Immediately all the other pigeons flew up flipping their wings as quickly as they could to escape from the clutches of the hunter.

Fahd had found his game. He carefully got out of the blanket and went to the pigeon. It was struggling to fly. He picked up the bird with his right hand and then tied the knot a little more tightly. Then he got a blade and started shredding a layer of feathers from its wings. This would prevent the bird from escaping easily. The bird was finally put inside a light aluminium cage and locked from outside.

"I had caught and tamed thirty-six pigeons at one time," he said with overbearing vanity. "I sold all of them three months ago. I got good price because they were young ones." As he said this, he shook a brown tin box, which was his penny bank. Not only did he sell pigeons, he also bought pigeons.

He spent so much time in the day tending his birds that he had come to imbibe their peculiar smell. None of the children in my classroom wanted to sit beside him because they complained that he gave off the smell of pigeons. This accusation was not completely untrue. Often the smell from his body was so intense and far-reaching that one could tell with eyes closed if he was around. There was no regular water supply in his neighbourhood and consequently, taking a bath was out of question. He remained dirty, like the earth. His arms and neck had long and running patches of dirt, accumulated over years of uncleanness and lack of personal hygiene.

Fahd had an elder brother and two elder sisters. His uncle, a fruit-seller, had two sons but their mother had died with her unborn child in their zilla hospital. Ever since that tragedy, the two sons were also raised in the same hut with Fahd's parents. The state of their family could only make me wonder. In our educated elite families, parents put up everything to raise just one or at most two children. Our families make long financial plans and calculations before thinking of having another child. But here in the slums, people had no such formula to decide whether another life would burden them. They did not have enough to eat every night. They did not have enough space in their rooms to sleep comfortably and worried that if the government would sweep them off their place, they would have to live on the pavements. Yet they accepted and embraced one another easily and gave them shelter. All out of humanity.

Children in the slums grew too quickly and it was not long before their hut did not have enough space for all the children. Every day, Fahd and the children took turns to go and live in their grandmother's place. They would return to their hut on the next day. Their grandmother was half-bent over her back, like an inverted L. Of everything else, she possessed an intense dislike for dirt and filth. When her grandchildren went to her place, she would scrub them for hours like a piece of garment. Surviving without water,

Fahd had come to fear water like a ghost. He yelled like an animal when he came into contact with it. Children in my class often threw water at him to make him scream.

Fahd's hygiene became a serious issue in the winter. He stopped going to his grandmother's house because she would force him to take a bath. For two months, his whole body smelled like an underground sewer pipe. It had become intolerable to keep him in class. After some time, I had to convince the *sevikas* to plan a surprise for him. I had tipped them fifty rupees to get them to do this without sounding anyone else in the school about it.

They had arranged two buckets of water behind the school toilet and a soap and scrubber. After the lunch break, they came to my class and asked Fahd to come outside. He obliged. They held the boy's hands and lifted him in the air. They took him to the toilet and washed him clean with soap and shampoo. His screams filled the whole air around the school. It was embryonic. When he came back to school, there was a deluge of laughter because he looked completely different, like a potato whose skin has been forcibly peeled off.

It was not long before I discovered that Fahd's real hero was none other than the Bollywood hero, Salman Khan. His hairstyle was like Salman's- long lines of jet black hair parted from the middle and dropping along sides of his eyes. It was in vogue then. His hairstyles however changed from one successful movie to another as his hero went on sporting new looks. There was a big bare-chested poster of Salman Khan pasted against the decaying wall of his house; it covered umpteen holes in between the bricks. There were also numerous smaller sized photos of Salman Khan all over the place- in the kitchen, under the TV set and one that he always carried in his pocket. The boy had memorized virtually every dialogue that made Salman Khan popular among the masses. When he spoke it seemed like it was Salman himself.

Fahd's real talent was, however, on the stage. All the twists and all the moves of Indian dance were contained in that frail poverty stricken body of his. He did not have a dance teacher. He borrowed DVDs for twenty rupees from a local shop right outside his slum. He would see the DVD on their TV's ever-flickering picture frame and pick up the dance from there. He could also pick up the dance moves of the heroines of Indian cinema. From Madhuri Dixit's 'Ek Do Tin' to Aishwarya Rai's 'Kajra Re'- his moves were second to none.

"When I grow up, I want to act in the movies," he expressed his desire to me. So he imitated their gait, their dialogues and their dance steps.

"If you have to act, the first thing you must know is how to dance and how to fight the villains. I can do both. When people will see in the theatres, they will not stop clapping."

Every year however his name was cancelled by the teachers from performing for the school's Annual Concert, first because of his age and second because he was an object of their dislike. Then the Annual Concerts started to get cancelled more often.

Fahd's star-studded life became real when I selected him for the Annual Concert of the school which was held in the middle of the academic year. He knew he was the best in the school, but being an epitome of modesty when it came to asking something for himself, he did not express his wish to perform. He wondered only in his mind whether or not I would pick him. When I broke the news to him, he jumped up from his seat and ran into my arms. He held me by my waist tightly with his hands around me and murmured a quick 'Thank You'.

I knew Fahd would not disappoint us but he needed to be disciplined. For a month, two teachers made him go through a rigorous regimen of practice to bring a touch of perfection to his talents. Two girls were also chosen to dance with him. They practiced endlessly in the afternoons over smashing hit songs from Bollywood and Marathi movies that were chosen for the concert.

When I reached school on the day of the concert, a large audience of children and parents from the slums and teachers from schools in the neighborhood had gathered on the school ground. Inside one of the classrooms on the ground floor, the performers were getting prepared. I saw the list of performers: Fahd was second from the last. The girls however had not arrived. One of them had reported sick and the other one, who was much younger, had not informed her parents about the concert. Consequently she did not make it to school.

The teachers who had put their sweat into the preparations were frustrated that all had gone into waste. The dresses had been bought but no one was there to put them on. They gruntingly decided to cancel our performance altogether. Almost immediately Fahd's eyes became teary. He turned away in disappointment and began to pack his bag. I felt sorry for him. Just then, an idea struck me. I went up to him and whispered in his ears. His eyes became full again and hugged me with his arms. As if he had lit a match.

Before his turn came, Fahd and I stood behind the stage. He was holding my hand tightly. I could feel his heart palpitating very fast. Then the announcement was made. He looked at me and I urged him on with my eyes, which may have assured him that everything was going to be fine. I patted him on his back twice and pushed him towards the stage. Once up there, he looked here and there and then snapped at the man who was playing the music on the loudspeakers.

His legs started moving and he let his body do what it needed to do, free to expand and contract in space, to soar and spin. About five minutes into the performance, it was time for his partners to dance. The music went on but Fahd scurried quickly behind the stage. He put a dupatta over his head and a readymade Marathi sari through whose legs he put his own. No one could have said that he was a boy in a girl's attire.

He got back on the stage and started performing the dance steps that were given to his partners. How he had mastered those steps in addition to his own was alluding. But he danced with his full spirit. His hips, his legs and his hands moved in the air in feminine style. His dark face was hidden under his choli but his magical smile set the stage on fire. When he raised the veil, his eyebrows leaped like a peacock in the rain. It was passionate and pretentious. The audience laughed and barracked him by standing up on their feet and clapping their hands in sheer adoration of the skilfulness with which he danced. Again he changed his dress to resemble his hero. Then again he was clad as a woman.

Fahd was performing a show of three dancers all by himself. It had turned into an amazing show. He did not seem to hear the music or feel his feet or get a sense of the audience. He was momentarily cut off from the world around him. Finally he fell down on the stage. The music had stopped by then. From the side, I saw him close his eyes and stretch his arms out. He was tired. The audience in the meanwhile had gone mad over his feat. They were possessed by gaiety and they cheered very loudly and requested him to repeat the show one more time.

When he stood up, he was panting heavily. He had no control. His legs were giving out. But the audience was adamant. The music began to play again and Fahd restarted. He performed the whole show again and the whole audience danced and whistled to his magically high spirit.

After the concert had ended, the teachers came to congratulate Fahd. For a boy who had never been appreciated in school, it had an unbelievable import on him. He looked dumbfounded that so many people were suddenly shaking his hands and praising him so thoroughly, but also bathed in a warm sense of accomplishment. I stood at a distance relishing his momentous joy.

NINE

When the window panes of my classroom broke in the monsoon, it revealed a sectional view of the neighbourhood, cut along the axis of the falling sky. Against a filthy, lifeless, tumbled-down background was painted an entanglement of irregular shaped poor huts, tilted over one another as if the ground under them had been deformed by an earthquake. The huts were surrounded by heaps of refuse and blocks of stones and bricks and open drains, ruined like the huts themselves. Smoke and sulphur surrounded the huts while the thin black lines of electricity dispelled the darkness inside these huts. Over nine tenths of the population in this neighbourhood lived in these shanties; their huts had no place for latrines and so they relieved themselves in the open air behind their huts. Their excrement dried in the sun, turned to dust and was inhaled by everyone along with the cool moist breezes of monsoon.

The congregation of these poor webs of houses stood separated by a ten-foot fence with rings of spikes and wires along its top. On the other side of the fence a five-storied building had been erected. Although the height of the building cast a tall overpowering shadow upon the slum huts, its anatomy did not bear any mark of grandeur to inspire reverence in the mind of an explorer. The building had no paint, but isolated parts of its inside walls seemed to carry old paints put up by the individual families who, in their tepid attempts, made only their own parts of the building appear more pleasant to the eye. Some had painted their part of the walls with red, some with pale yellow, some green. Others probably could not afford that. Every floor was surrounded on all sides by verandas that served as a place to hang clothes onto the outside of the building. A retinue of doors separated by about a feet were perched against the walls. Nothing inside was visible. The doors were so small and dark inside that it resembled the rat holes that existed throughout the school. It made me wonder how entire families could fit in to these holes.

Ayan lived in one of those holes. Unlike the other boys, he was tiny in size, just enough to pass through a hole. He was in fact so little that I believe he panicked repeatedly about the possibility that one day he might not be visible to others anymore. He first came to my class three weeks after the academic year had begun. I could not avoid noticing this thin, desperate boy with sick yellow protruding eyes. He couldn't have been more than four and a half feet tall. His head looked like a giant coconut, heavier than the rest of his body. It had been shaved down almost to the scalp and the remaining layer of hair was polished with a thick film of oil.

He did not have many friends or enemies but he was a target of the older looking boys in the class who would bully him and often beat him without any pity whatsoever. At times, when he was not their outright target, he ended up being a misfortunate casualty of gang violence and ruthless infighting. It broke my soul to see how defenceless he was. The boys in the school who lived in the neighbourhood harassed him outside the gates of the school. On several days, they had chased him upto his home and threatened to beat him up. Being shy, he never told me why.

Given the close proximity of Ayan's home from the school, I often thought of visiting his house but I had not quite found the time until he suffered his most fatal injury in school. Three boys from the seventh class got into a row with him and in a fit of rage, knocked his head with a cricket bat. Ayan got four stitches. He was advised to stay at home for a week. When two weeks passed and he did not come back to school, I decided out of a growing concern to pay him a visit.

A rough and partly-cemented path led me to the entrance of his building. Such buildings were ample in the slums of the Peth. All of them had the same history. They were built upon a slum land whose residents have been uprooted by money or force. Once a group of poor had been removed, another group would encroach and settle inside these buildings. Living in a building gave this new group of poor a better social standing than living in a slum.

Third floor, fourth door. That was my address. Garbage was littered all around the way to the entrance and the staircase that led me up stank with the heavy pungent smell of urine. The staircase was completely dark and the moment I had set foot on the inside, I felt as though I had lost my eyesight. It was deficiently illuminated at places by narrow gleams of light that had squeezed though pieces of newspaper pasted against occasional ventilators. At one corner, flashes of electricity twinkled inside an electric meter box whose casing had been opened. It cast a little light onto the staircase and with its help, I saw a cat running down the right side. Climbing this flight of stairs would have been as precarious as walking on a sheet of ice. After every step, I had to wait and think of how far to stretch my foot again so as not to make a false step. I kept my left hand on the wall on the side so that I could balance my weight and prevent falling in this darkness. It was astounding how the people in this building had been used to this inconceivable cecity that filled the daily path of their lives.

On every floor a narrow corridor with open doors stretched along the length. I could see, by straining my eyes in the indistinct light that poured out of these doors, that several men and women were sleeping on the corridors. The sound of their snoring echoed though the dark passages. Along with the resident sleepers, a few dogs had also discovered a resting ground at every turn of the stairs, away from the afternoon heat. I had to be extra-careful not to step on them.

With some difficulty, I alighted on the third floor and turned left. The corridor was thumping with the heavy chattering and clamour of men and women and children. The noises came from inside the rooms. After three doors came Ayan's door. There was no plank to cover the door, only a frame and a curtain hanging from the frame to veil the room from the outside. There was no bell, so I had to call Ayan by name. No one answered at first, but then a beautiful little face peeped outside. On seeing me, she pulled the rest of the curtain aside and revealed herself.

"*Ammi*? Come outside." This was his sister, I guessed from the similarity of their appearances. She was only a little taller than Ayan and probably of the same age. From inside, the coarse voice of her Ammi asked her to let me in.

The room was hardly ten feet long and four feet wide with an open door on the opposite side exposing the outer veranda. Daylight fell inside the room with violent intensity much like a waterfall coming down a steep mountain. My eyes rested upon the back side of the school building. It looked almost like a water colour painting tinted with a grey background.

On the right wall of the room, a framed photograph of the symbolic Black Stone from the Grand Mosque of Mecca hung in pride. A bulb was above it. There were no other lights in the room. The wall were designed with cracks. There was no paint anywhere. The ceiling was infected with worms. A bed stood at one corner against the wall with a TV set; an old wooden cupboard and a pedestal fan was placed near it. That completed all the furnishings in the room.

Ayan's mother was cooking in the veranda on a small stove, kept on the floor to which a gas cylinder was dangerously attached. She was surrounded by three young girls, of varying heights, who were cutting potatoes, onions and vegetables. Another girl was sewing clothes at the doorstep. She looked much older than the rest. As soon as their Ammi saw me, she glanced at her girls speaking in symbols. They left their work and rushed along the veranda, only to come back after a minute clad from head to toe in burqa. They again resumed their work as assiduously as before.

Ayan's mother came inside the room and started pulling the cloth that was spread over the cot by the ends so that it looked ironed. I sat on the bed when she was done. "Good to see you sir. Ayan's *abbu* has taken him to the doctor. They would be home in a few minutes. Do you want to take anything?" she asked very hospitably. I insisted that there was no need for anything, but she did not listen to me. She would not leave me because I had come for the first time. She called her elder daughter, Alfiya, who was stitching the torn ends of a salwar and asked her to get milk to make tea for me.

"We cannot afford milk for so many people in our family," she said smilingly, "So, we keep it only for guests."

Alfiya pulled the veil of her burqa so that only her eyes were visible and went downstairs.

I tried to start a conversation with Ayan's mother. She told me they had six children- five girls and one boy. The entire family had been living in a slum in Lohiyanagar for a long time until they had been uprooted from there by the slum lords. Then they settled here. There they had only a small hut in an over-populated slum. The hut was half the size of this one. There was no water, no bathrooms and so little place inside the hut that all the family members used to sit outside all day long. She tried to give me rough directions of roads to the place where they used to live before. I knew the place well enough to imagine how tiny their slum-hut might have been. How so many people could eat, sleep, cook and live in such a small space like that, I thought for a while.

One of her girls had finished slicing the onions and declared her completion with a rather faint enthusiasm. Her Ammi went outside and took the preparation from her and put it on the burning oil in the stove. Immediately the whole room filled up with the intense smell of onions, bringing quick tears to my eyes. I closed my eyes and kept rubbing them until a familiar voice sounded in the room.

"Sir, you have come to our house. I cannot believe this." It was Ayan's voice, but full of excitement. I haven't heard him speak with so much delight before.

When I finally opened my eyes, I saw him. His gaze was lit up with a glint of joy. He still had bandages clipped to his head but the rest of him looked in much better shape. There was a man now standing right opposite me, leaning against the wall. He was Ayan's father, a dark-skinned wiry man, probably in the forties. His yellow eyes were haggard and cavernous and his hair was thick and curly with sideburns that sank down along his face to continue into his black and grey beard. Once the drizzling sound of the onions had faded away, he began to talk but unlike the boy, he threw his words belligerently at me.

"I have only one son and this is what happens to him in school. He is afraid all the time, I cannot see him suffering in this condition anymore. The school does not look after our children properly when they are there."

He walked to and fro as he spoke. "My son says that if goes back to school, he will get beaten up by the boys again. This time, he overcame his injuries but what if such an incident happens again? Last year, a boy had bitten him in the ear. So much blood had oozed from his ears that he was in a hospital for ten days. When I learned about the boy who had done that to him, I went to his slum with my people and beat him and his father up." I had seen that mark on

Ayan's ears but now I knew where they came from. "I have only one son and I cannot see his suffering," he repeated.

As he calmed down, the room became silent again. He looked at the floor, despaired and concerned. I looked outside, staring at the endless black palls of smoke that gently widened far beyond into the world, thinking of them in my mind.

In the meanwhile, Alfiya had come back with a packet of milk. Handing it over to her mother, she opened the cupboard and took out a heap of clothes from the base and threw it at her sister. I watched the little girl immerse the clothes into a bucket of water and detergent and start twisting them with the all the force stored in her small hands.

One of the girls came from the corridor with a plate full of biscuits and sweets and glass of water. She was the one who had answered the door when I came. Like her mother, her father would not listen. "Sir, you have come here for the first time. We don't have such guests like you coming to our place every day. We must do at least this much." Picking up the instructions from her father, she handed me the cup and plate. I asked her which class she was studying in.

"*Chauthi*," she replied almost breathlessly, not looking at me. She looked much older than Ayan but studied at a lower grade.

"Which school do you go to?"

"You go to the corridor and help your mother," her father interrupted her and she quietly walked to the corridor and stood behind the corner of the door, showing only her face. "There is an Urdu medium school here in the neighbourhood. Only three buildings away. All my girls study there."

"Why an Urdu-medium school? Why doesn't she come to school like Ayan?" I had asked this question bluntly.

"Sir, let it go," her father said, twitching his lips. "She is a girl. What would she do by studying anyways? It is not going to help her in any way. We want to keep her in school for one more year only. After that she will stop going to school and work in the house." The girl stood there immovably, silently listening to her father's opinions about her worthlessness.

"Why? Do you not like going to school?" I asked her, looking away from her father and tried to put up a cheerful smile. "Do you not want to study more and become someone someday?" I wanted to hear her speak. She looked at me blankly as if I was the first person ever to have asked her that question. She only nodded her head, which could have meant both ways, and began to twist the corner of the veil of her burqa with her fingers.

"Sir," interrupted her father, "Hamare yaha aisa chalta hain. Our girls aren't required to study and go ahead much also. Then why should we unnecessarily spend our money for their education when they are not going to earn a living and they are not going to be with us forever. Look at my son. He has been so bright right from the beginning. He will make money and look after us. That is why I have put him into English-medium school."

He spoke in an almost pragmatic but indifferent tone but his words perplexed me from inside. The reality of this family wriggled my neck like a bug, eliminating the possibility of its victim to come up with a better argument to counter him. I glanced at the girl once again- she was now sitting with her head and soul dipped into preparing the vegetables for her family's meal. I took my eyes away instantly. If I had stared at her a little longer in time, I would have retired with a permanently broken heart.

It seemed to me that as she'd grown up, her ineptitude had also ballooned. She wore it over her like a second layer of skin, carrying it with her under her burqa. My patience was failing me. How would she have felt all these years, I thought? Did she also think of herself as worth nothing?

The irony was that while Ayan himself was going slower than others in my class, his father continued to live under a brittle impression about his son's intelligence. His previous year's grade book contained countless zeroes and I knew that even if he worked hard for the rest of the year he would still be so behind many students, that he barely had a chance this year to catch up with the class.

But more than I had ever felt sorry for Ayan's plight, I was now bottomed by the fate of his five sisters. I could not grasp their father's contradictions. I argued for some time before I realized that to him these little girls were like life's follies, best when forgotten. They were things of the past, which had ceased to bear any existence in the present. And yet they continued to exude a beauty and an innocence that spoke of abiding happiness regardless of the silent humiliation they were facing.

I would have liked to count Ayan among one of my first major victories. When he came to my class, Ayan could barely write and read a few common words in English, mostly two or three letters long, and identify numbers only upto 99. All of this had taken him several years to memorize. The teachers who had been with him in the years gone by had rejected him as a complete failure.

"You cannot teach him anything," one teacher told me about him. "This boy doesn't have anything inside him." The teachers thought it was best to ignore his presence and move on with the rest. But they had made it a point to remind him of his regression every now and then.

Ayan told me that he was also attending an Arabic school. He went there after returning home from Mahadeo Govind Ranade. All this could have only added to the infinite confusion playing out inside his mind.

Ayan's problems in academics were genuinely alarming though. Going through his exercise books one night, I only had a faint suspicion of an overwhelming difficulty with him. Within a matter of days however I found out that he could not understand anything of anything unless one drew pictures alongside the written words. This made teaching him all the more difficult. Weeks passed before I managed to teach him how to visualize and make sense of the symbols that represented numbers and blocks, add and subtract numbers and form words from pictures. Phonetics was the hardest thing for him to grasp and he failed again and again when it came to remembering the sounds that alphabets made when combined. Often he would simply stare blankly at my face, unable to speak a single word, putting my patience to test. It irritated me at times, yet to get that one word of his mouth, I almost threw myself into this new challenge, putting all of my creative energies -from flashcards to ice-cream sticks and all kinds of household objects.

This exercise went on for about three months before Ayan showed signs of progress. His speed and accuracy of reading English improved, coupled with his English scores that began to jump little by little after every class test, while his Math scores ticked forward, albeit slowly. He would watch the class tracker every time to see where he stood. I found that to be an encouraging sign. But while this may have been the first year when he shown evidence of progress in academics, I could not be sure whether he would be able to remember all of what I had taught. Yet I was pleased that he had started to make up for the time he had lost in school.

I began going to his house more frequently, teaching him as much as I could through the evenings. His mother felt grateful that I afforded him with a privilege that nobody else in the family had. At home, Ayan was a very fortunate child. He was treated by the family exactly in the way his name had been chosen. It meant God's gift. Indeed after the *anathema* of five girls, the family had felt truly blessed when a boy was born, which had earned him the family's love and attention so much so that he had become an overly protected boy. He was the subject of their breakfast and dinner table talk. All their energies, money and time were invested in his future. His childhood was so isolated from the neighbourhood that the outside world was literally unknown to him. He was living inside a box that was his home.

His eldest sister, Anum was in an Arabic school for all these years until she was forced to quit school when it was felt that education was no longer a necessity. After leaving school, Anum put her time into learning the art of stitching clothes and cooking at her mother's hands. The other girls also divided the household chores equally after their school-time, sacrificing their dolls, whose dismembered bodies I saw lying at the corner of their room in tin box. At night they often got pounded with utensils by their father for being a curse onto the family.

Anum's role in the family had long ceased to be that of a teenage girl. Instead, she had been forced into the life of a servant, waking up at six in the morning with her mother and working till midnight. She went to sleep after her mother. This draconian routine of household chores had made her frail, yet she seemed to me to possess the obsessions of a slave. Whenever she had free time, she would devote herself to putting their world in order- folding clothes, sweeping the floor, dusting the corners, picking up trash- and then repeating the same tasks even though it was unnecessary. She had also unknowingly become a mother even before she was six years old. Ayan had been brought up and nourished by his eldest sister because their mother was too weak to get up after childbirth. She had fed him, bathed him, stitched his clothes, took him to school and put him to sleep.

I had seen an old picture of his sister hidden inside a page of his book. Anum was in the picture, she was very small then. She had hair only upto her neck but it was upbraided and clumsy, left free over her face to hide her flaming pair of blue-green eyes. In the picture, she was smiling luminously like a sunflower facing the sun. She held a baby in her hand, Ayan, who looked like an silent extension of herself. He was only a few months old when the photograph was taken. In a photographic moment of triumphal joy, she was raising him in the air like a trophy. Using both her small arms, she held him tightly. Since then, the selfless soul of the child had shared the family's pride and happiness at the birth of a boy. I could not take my eyes off the photograph. It told me so much about the girl.

Ayan protected the picture with his heart and soul. Anum was his first mother and, later on, his teacher. In a way, she came to occupy the greater portion of his inner world of beliefs. He studied at home under her supervision because by far she was the most educated in the family. Now out of school, she fulfilled her own desire to study by teaching her younger brother.

Ayan's father did nothing much to make a stable income. Some people in the neighbourhood said that the nightmare of seeing the birth of one girl after another when all he wanted every time from his wife was a boy had cracked his brain up from inside. He used to abuse his wife calling her names because she could only give birth of girls. He worked here and there for other people, doing mostly backbreaking manual labour but only as a part-time worker. For a month or two he drove another man's auto rickshaw, then worked at an oil mill, then pulled carts with grocery from one market to another. But his heavy drinking and hot-blooded nature got him into trouble with the job contractors. Their income being irregular and below what was needed to substantiate their most elementary needs, Ayan's mother kept the family alive by making paper bags out of old newspapers. She was frequently driven to beg her neighbours and relatives for some money, promising to pay back as soon as her husband found new work. Those who knew her conditions knew her too well to lend anything.

There was one woman in their building however who knew how to turn the gears of her neighbour's plight. A social worker, she lived three doors and one floor below her family, and worked for the girl children in the neighbourhood. She ran a small centre with the generous support of a few wealthy donors in the city, Ayan's mother had told me during one of my visits. She had noted that I came regularly to the building, she had caught a glimpse of which room I went to and she had discovered perhaps the biggest difference that set me apart from Ayan's family: the difference of religion.

She had advised them that they do not let me come to their house because they had five young girls and a well-dressed English-speaking man visiting them frequently was not a healthy thing. Such people have pestiferous intentions, she had warned them. It was a sign of danger- people *like me* would say all sorts of things to disturb the minds of their girls and lure them away from the family. It would bring them great shame and rejection in the community. When Ayan's mother requested me, I was instantly stifled by the insanity of her misinterpretations and I decided to halt my visits to their building.

For a year now, this social worker had been devising a solution for Anum's future. The poor thing had one quality that made her priceless in the eyes of everyone: her splendid looks. With silk-like semi-golden tresses, pink cheeks and blue-green eyes, she resembled nothing less than a doll. No one seemed to have noticed this faster than her and she had discreetly brought up a proposal that she knew her wise, pragmatic neighbour would not turn down. She convinced Anum's mother to dispatch his eldest daughter to the custody of a *rich* family in Bombay as a domestic help. She had made the agreement with care and secrecy and paid the family fifty thousand rupees right away. Indeed it was a lot of money, to relieve them of having to go through the trouble of buying food only in minute quantities every day. Ayan had confessed this secret to me, almost staggering me with a rush of emotions. "Tell Ayan, I love him immensely," is what she said before going.

As much I would have liked to prevent Anum from being sacrificed, I could not however do anything but make almost trembling guesses from here.

The fate of his sister, Ayan's only companion in the world had sent up vapours of maddening incense before the eye of his mind. It was like a sandstorm or an avalanche. He seemed deformed by a sort of wounded and fallen hope, whose outburst was only lurking in the offing. Two weeks later, it showed its teeth. I had gone to the staffroom to prepare a list for the upcoming scholarship examination for my class. I was perusing through the class register when a boy from the fourth standard came running in and informed me that a terrible combat had happened in the class. Ayan had fallen out with Divya. Upon hearing Divya's name, I sank. This girl anchored a pervading rancour for the Muslim students, which got her into frequent trouble with the boys in the Urdu-medium. This time, she dissed at Ayan and his sisters by calling them *dukkar*, which meant swine. Somehow she knew about his sisters. For some time, they pelted at each other with fireballs of obscenities until he could no longer stand the insult she had made to his sisters. He dashed out of the classroom bustling in fury.

Five minutes later he had come back with a plank of wood that he had taken out from a bench. With that plank, he attacked Divya and hit her face. Her nose opened almost instantly while blood dripped down her face like a tap of water left open. Then he hit again but this time, he had raised the plank high above his head and brought it down over the girl's shoulders.

A part of plank came off from the side and fell on the floor. The girl had become unconscious already. She was doused in blood but the other children dared to go near Ayan to stop him. He had entered a paroxysm of fury. They saw a conscious unrest seething in his veins. He had done his job but he stood near his victim watching her, like an animal inspecting its kill, with his eyes burning with the fire of some phantasmal ruthlessness. The whole onslaught had lasted in only about three minutes. I rushed to my classroom and pushed the boy aside from behind. Divya was lying motionless on the floor. I picked her up and with another teacher sped to the hospital.

When I returned home that day, it was six in the evening. I stood leaning over the railing of my balcony, thinking hard over the incident that had happened in the day. Like a soldier who has survived a war but lost everything, I brooded over the destruction that lay before my eyes. At a distance, I could see the slums protruding its arms into the far horizons like a jellyfish. A world that was becoming more unequal with time. The air was filled with the sound of Adan coming from a mosque nearby.

My tea tasted bitter.

Slowly, the view of the encompassing city lit with yellow and white lights that lay before me began to moisten away in the streams falling from my eyes. Coldness spread all over me and I surrendered again to grief and an insurmountable loss: both Ayan and Divya survived the tragedy but they were never seen in the school again.

TEN

Spring came to Mahadeo Govind Ranade with the promise of renewal and rebirth, as the redolence of its myriad blossoms filled our hearts with the hope of new beginnings and endless possibilities. The fresh fragrance of a new awakening moistened the air as the neighbourhood bade farewell to the fog-filled winter of struggles. It was the day before Makar Sankranti, the eve of the arrival of a spring of joy.

I was in the neighbourhood, strolling through streets which were richly laid with men and women and children, bargaining with shopkeepers and hawkers whose shops were decorated with kites, flowers and ornaments. Little boys were rolling their hands through the bundles of silk to examine their tensile strength and durability. I stood at the side of one shop and watched as the shopkeepers kept on bragging about the quality of the materials hoping to entice the children to pay a higher price. The children pretended to know everything about the fabric and the lift of the kites. "This material is not good enough," said one of them. "Have you seen *that* shopkeeper's kites? They are so strong," said another and moved to the next shop. The shopkeeper kept on calling out to them from behind, but they would not pay any heed. The shopkeeper however had to give up soon, because another group of boys had already gathered before his cart.

I walked down the street where the shops had poured onto the main road. They were selling adornments, sweets and utensils. The shops behind them were selling *laddus,* turmeric powder and saris. Red, green, yellow, blue, black and a thousand combinations of colours to appeal to every possible human emotion.

A hand tapped me on my back.

"Sir, you are here?" said a familiar voice.

I turned around and saw Rahi carrying his little sister in his arms. "I can't believe this," he said. His eyes were struck with amazement. He was just so startled to see me at the markets. I smiled thinking that in his innocent mind it had never occurred that a teacher also existed outside of school.

"Well I was passing by the place and stopped for a while," I told him.

"Will you help me a little then? I want to buy a few kites and *manja* for tomorrow. But Guddi is not coming down from my arms. Can you hold her while I shop?"

I held the crying toddler as she kicked her legs. We walked to the upper end of the street. He took me into a shop, which though had a tiny door, was by no way tiny inside. A hundred kites were hanging outside the entrance from a rope and several hundreds more piled inside.

Rahi's innocent eyes were fixated to those kites which were the most colourful and gorgeous to look at, not the ones which could win him the battle of kites. He wanted to show off the beauty of his kites to his friends in the neighbourhood. The shopkeeper perhaps understood that and went on showing one kite after another, all dazzling with designs, and telling him that these kites were the rarest of the lots that have come this year to the bazaar. One would not get such variety elsewhere in the city.

He stood there like a mixed-up child, not knowing which ones to buy. He wished his mother had given him enough money to buy all the kites in that shop. The shopkeeper, wanting to make a deal with the boy, suggested that he could select as many kites as he wanted to and he would give him a discount after that. Excited by the offer, Rahi quickly sat down on the floor of the shop and began sifting through the bundles of kites.

The shopkeeper smiled at me and said, "I know this boy very well. He stays a few blocks from my house. We live in the same chawl. I know his family well. He loves flying kites. Do you know how often he gets beaten up at home because of his kites? Yet he saves money little by little every day of the year and then uses his savings to buy kites. With him, I can always be lenient about prices."

Rahi did not hear a word of what was said about him. He was perusing through the rhombus of his imaginations. He selected ten of them and put them on the table. "I will pay you the rest as soon as I can. For the time being, I have only hundred. Will you let me have these?" he said. The shopkeeper nodded and said, "These kites are strong, but remember that the kite-flyer needs to be stronger than his kite." Rahi smiled.

It was time for *manja* now. The boy knew a place where they sold the deadliest type of *manja*, a special variety imported from China. The person who sold it was found underneath a building on the rear side of the market. Again a tiny unlit shop in a lane where not more than one person could walk into at a time.

"Unless he knows you personally, he will not give you that *manja* for cheap," Rahi said in a way that seemed like he was trying to show me what an important customer he was. "I have a deal with him."

Before leaving for home, Rahi invited me to his home for the kite flying festival next day.

On the day of Sankranti, the Peth did not wear the badge of poverty, and light and high beauty reached beyond the usual shadows of its dim huts. People painted the house facades and doors, window frames and shutters, balcony rails and decorative details appeared like variations on a theme, using saturated pastel colours, mainly on wood, but also on plastered walls, as well as on corrugated steel and other building materials. The streets were the decked up like a garden of many flowers where children were running about with plates full of sweets and kites. The talk of the games seemed to be on every lip like a prayer or a song. Their eyes were posited to the sky where a rainbow of kites was meddling with each other. The children on the streets were eagerly watching the conflicts of the kites with rib-tickling tension, hoping to see some kite fall off the sky and rest over the electric cables so that they could run after and catch. Their hopes were realized every minute as kites were cut by other kites. Once a kite fell off the firmament, it belonged to no one anymore and the children rushed after it with excitement, wanting to claim it before someone else could. The prize of that kite was too high to let go. It was the emblem of joy, victory and escape to which man and child rejoiced equally.

Making my way through this pocket of joy, I reached Rahi's house in Raviwar Peth. The door of his small house was richly decorated with garlands and there were several people standing at the entrance. Rahi's little sister who was on my lap yesterday was decorating the entrance of the house with a variety of colors and chandan. She recognized me immediately and ran inside to call her mother.

"You are Rahi's teacher, am I right? Please come in."

She took me inside. There was one small room outside and a room inside could be seen from the door where there was a kitchen and the shed of a bathroom. The house wasn't big enough for even four people but somehow this large crowd of guests had fitted themselves in, like a bundle of sticks tied together. Rahi's mother introduced me to the people sitting in the room.

"Today is a special day in our family. We are celebrating Haldi Kumkum today. Rahi's aunt has organised this festival for the married women in our family and in the neighbourhood. We are waiting for them to come." At that moment, Rahi's father, a tall dark man in his forties came out with a basket full of laddus and upon seeing me, he put one of the laddus into my mouth.

"*Tilgul ghya, god god bola*," he said, which, as I learned later, meant that one has to accept these laddus and say sweet words to each other. Rahi's mother introduced me to him as his teacher, hearing which his father tried to put another til laddu into my mouth.

"The til laddu makes people forget the ills of the past and to look forward to happiness and well-being," he said.

I asked where Rahi was. The little boy was on the roof with his kites. His father showed me the way. A small wooden ladder, with its planks dangling downwards, led to the roof of the hut. Seeing how precarious climbing this ladder would be, I asked for help. Rahi hauled me with both his hands while his father pushed me up from below until I was on the roof.

The boy was on the roof with his four cousins. They had a stack of kites tied to the television antenna on the roof. All their hands were taped with black-tape. This was done to prevent their soft hands from being hurt by the *manja*.

"Last year, my elder brother was severely injured by *manja*. His palms were bleeding and he had become senseless. From this year, we are all wearing this tape to keep our hands safe."

Rahi and the boys had teamed up against the kite flyers on the roof of a five-storeyed building that stood at about two hundred metres from their hut. The enthusiastic screams and the yells of the children filled the air as each team tried to bring down the other's kites. It was a savage battle in the skies. The boys would run to the edge of the roof and run back excitedly, all the while handling the *manja* with great acuity, when they saw victory over the rival kites.

As I watched the games of kites, I drifted back in time. I was a nine year old again. To me, flying kites symbolized a culture and a religion in itself. I used to stand behind my uncles and brothers and pick up their tips on just about everything there was to learn about flying. In the early days, I would only hold the silk for them while they tried to lift the kites up in the air. Naturally I learned to fly kites when I was a little older. I remembered how hard I tried every afternoon to lift the kites up. It had taken me many months to lurch it upwards and when I had finally succeeded, I was saluted with a trumpet of squalls and a burst of cheers. That was the custom.

"Today, I have cut four kites but I lost three myself," Rahi said and heralded me back from the past. "Those boys on the building can fly better than I do. Their kites are also stronger. I try to keep away from them but they keep coming at my kites." He was running back and forth the roof to steer his kite and direct it in the direction of the air current.

Then suddenly, we saw a kite come staggering down and stop at a branch of a tree bending down over their roof. Rahi's younger brother, not more than six years of age, who still hadn't earned the proficiency to fly kites himself, saw the game and rushed immediately to grab it. He climbed up the wobbly branch, carefully balancing his weight with his small limbs and tried hard to reach out to the kite with a hook attached to the top of a bamboo stick. He aimed at it but his small hands would not reach. Not willing to give up, he leaned his body a little further every time until his hand just got to the kite.

It seemed to me that the kite was not just a toy for him, but a thing which carried his incarcerated soul into the invisible regions of the sky of freedom. Like a bird with big wings. He ran back quickly and inspected the value of his catch. A glum disappointment came down upon his face. The kite had a hole in the middle. This one is worth nothing and his brothers would not be happy seeing his catch.

Guests were coming to Rahi's family throughout the day. They were mostly women, some of whom were accompanied by their husbands. They were putting a pinch of haldi and kumkum on the face of a young woman sitting on a mat. She was dressed in exquisite red bridal sari with gold decorations and ornaments all over her. I was told that she was Rahi's aunt. Rahi's mother and grandmother were sitting beside her.

The ceremony started with the women sitting in a circle on the floor and singing in which I obviously couldn't participate. I was instead handed with a plate of food which bore the colours of haldi and kumkum: yellow semolina cooked with spices and orange sweet carrots cooked in milk. One of the older women was creating the rhythm with brass jingles, which made a fine soothing tune. The singing then moved into prayers dedicated to a shrine of Krishna and Laxmi, their gods.

After the prayers, Rahi's aunt gave out gifts and sweets made of sesame to the women who were blessing her. "Sesame is a warm seed which in the winter that we have here will give you warmth and a good feeling," Rahi's mother told me and put a mark of haldi on my forehead. "This haldi is not just for the women, we put it on men also."

She insisted that if I stayed till the evening, I will get to play a game where men and women splash turmeric on one another.

Then Rahi's grandmother brought the most important guest of the day: the new-born boy in their family. He was Rahi's cousin. The little boy, barely a few months old, was dressed up like Krishna with a paper crown and wreaths. He was placed on a blue, round, small blanket and then a tray with a candle, a little box containing the spices and something that looked grainier like broken rice, a golden ring and sesame biscuit was swayed around and above him.

Vermillion was used for a dot on the forehead the grains were sprinkled over his head, the ring touched his temples and was swayed over the head and then he was fed a tiny bit of biscuit that seemed to confuse him most.

The resplendent culture of this Maharashtrian family was a tremendous thing to watch. The whole family and the neighbourhood had come together to bath in the downpour of blessings of a new season. It was my first time and even though I was still a novice at the dialects spoken in the neighbourhood, yet I felt very closely drawn to them.

On the outside, children were still staring at the skies for the kites to fall. The little ones in the family looked as excited as the birds in the spring. Their unquenchable thirst for festivity reflected in their eyes. They were the ones who were also enjoyed the most, jumping around, running and boasting about their conquests in the sky. They would go into the kitchen area every five or ten minutes and steal *laddus* for each other by hiding them under their shirts and slipping out without anyone noticing. The song and dances continued till the light faded into the horizons.

I decided to take leave. Rahi's father accompanied me.

"Rahi needs a teacher just like you, sir," he began with an emotional voice as we came out onto the lane outside. "We never had a teacher who talked to us or called us to talk about our son. It feels so nice when a teacher comes to us. There should be more teachers like you in the school. Otherwise our children would never do anything good in their lives.

"We did not have much by the way of an education. I left school in 3rd class and began to work and his mother read till 5th class. But we want him to complete school and we try to do everything we can for him. That is what I always tell him- education comes first, everything else can come later. I tell him all the time: if you study, you can go to college and then you can get a job and you can get out of the poor situation we are in today. If you don't, you will lose everything one day."

His voice was pitched with an imperturbable commitment that he showed towards his children's education. "We never bought a TV set in our house because it would hamper his education. His mother used to put the latch on the door from inside so that he could go out to meet the local boys in the evenings. But I ask you, sir, what is he going to learn if nothing is being taught in school? Even when he was at home, he did not know what to do, what to learn. We may not be able to read his books or write but we could understand that he was not learning anything. I tell you, sir, nothing will really change unless these school teachers change."

He suddenly stopped and held both my hands together tightly. "We have all our trust upon you. You have changed our son so much. Previously, Rahi never used to talk of school. He had all sorts of distractions. But now he says he enjoys going to school, he comes back home and reads his books throughout the evening. He tries to speak in English all the time. It makes us feel good. When I see him do better day by day, I often wish that I had completed school myself as well." I felt a warm, peaceful sensation flood my chest.

Jaunting through the unknown worlds of these families, I found myself beginning to forge new kinds of relationships with so many people that I had never known before. I learned to share in their hopes, fears, doubts and joys, to trust them and to find my own space in them. Quite unwittingly perhaps, I was becoming like them. Over the following few weeks and months, I visited Rahi's hut so many more times that his mother had come to treat me like her own brother. Every time I showed up at their doorstep to meet the young boy, the family suffused me into an ocean of affection and respect and added small fractions of an almost effable joy to my soul. His mother proved to be very helpful- she taught me many different ways to cook fish and vegetables.

The warmth of this family always overwhelmed me with all that was beautiful about the neighbourhood. My roots spread deep and wide to the extent that it had almost become my second home, with my heart content and always humbly accepting the care and kindness that a place of this kind had to offer. I knew each lane, each by-lane, each street, each square and almost each building. I bought all my necessaries and supplies from the shops in the neighbourhood and ate at the same places where my children ate.

Unable to read and write properly, Rahi's father had asked me to help him fill out an application form to open the family's first account with the State Bank. A bank account that symbolised a state of well-being and abundance in a neighbourhood of poorness. A little favour however had earned me a reputation that, as I discovered very soon, reached farther than I could possibly imagine. The next time I was in their house, several men from the neighbourhood had flocked outside Rahi's home requesting me to fill out their forms as well. Rahi's father had spread the word. People had come for help with bank accounts, passport applications, ration card, post office accounts, and school admission forms and at the end of each assignment I was invariably presented with their earnest loyalty.

The other thing that I was learning from this poor, beleaguered and alienated neighbourhood was the art of making *bidis* with hand which was the one common source of living for almost all the men and women here. In every single house, people kept numerous baskets of loose tobacco leaves grained into powder form and the women in these houses would start out from early morning to bind the tobacco into rolled paper. Some of the men also did odd jobs like carpentry or tailoring, besides making *bidis* in the evening.

By frequently staying in the neighbourhood, I had earned the privilege to visit the home of another student, Om who lived only a few houses away from Rahi's. Om was growing up without a father and his mother made a living for her two sons by selling hand-made *bidis* to the local distributors. It was in her hands that I became slightly proficient in making *bidis*.

The ground floor of their shaky wooden house had a go-down for food grains and the other rooms on the upper floor were occupied by several other families. More than ten women were sitting outside on the long narrow dust-clad corridor, making *bidis*. I hurdled over these workers, leaping every time with care so as not to spill the tobacco, until I reached the second last door of the corridor.

Stepping into their room, I was immediately told of the state of insufferable privation of this family. The room, which lacked many things other than space, resembled a prison cell that had been deserted by its inmate; its walls were dark and dank and crumbling under the attack of pests and rainwater. The wall on the right of their door had a line of hooks pinned to it to hang utensils. They had only a countable few. A small stove and a bottle of kerosene was right under it. There was also a small-sized thin mattress laid out on the floor for sleeping and a few notebooks from school lying at the corner.

Unlike Rahi's house, they did not have a gas connection, a difference that said more about this family's wretched plight than perhaps anything else. The other things that were in the room were a faded photo of a young man, whom I recognised at once as Om's father by the striking similarity in their faces, and a photo of the child god Krishna trying to steal butter out from a bowl with his little hands.

Inside this airless room, his mother was busy at her work while Om, her elder son, was assisting her with the powder and the threads and her younger son was playing with a spinning top outside.

It became obvious to me that I was the first teacher to have come to their house for Om's mother was very surprised to see me there. I thought she was a little scared, and so was Om. She calmed down only after she felt completely ascertained that her son had done nothing wrong in school. I sat down beside her in curiosity and asked her to teach me the art of her profession.

"We make about 1000 *bidis* a day and get 55 rupees for it," she told me. "It takes almost a whole day to make 1000 *bidis*." She had a long greenish brown paper with a scrubby surface and a rectangular piece of stone to use as a measuring piece to cut the paper. She then poured the tobacco powder onto the pieces of paper neatly cut out and roll the paper up. To make it taut, she used white silk to tie it. Her hands moved with such an astounding speed and dexterity that it seemed to me that her nerves had been trained only for this kind of crucial and exacting work.

Even her son Om was immensely skilled at making *bidis*, but with his little hands he could only make about a hundred a day, five and a half rupees more for the family. His little brown hands looked scarred by the ceaseless abrasion with tobacco. But he was determined to help his mother with the work and had not even taken off his school uniforms before putting his hands into work. Apparently, this was why he always found a reason to excuse himself from attending my extra-tutoring classes after school.

His mother however did not want him to make *bidis* all day for she feared that her son would get the same bad lung that took his father away. Their lungs were weak from constantly inhaling the dust that came off from the *bidis* and none of them lived long lives in these neighbourhoods, she told me. Om's chest had already begun to become narrow, his breath was short and stinking and his back crooked.

Om's mother described to me how fragile and frail their living conditions were. Surviving on a shoestring budget implied that on many days, she would have to go hungry because there wasn't enough money coming in from the trade for many times in the year the company would delay their payments. She could not do anything else on the side because she had never known anything else besides making *bidis*. She could not go back to work in the fields in her village because there was no one left out there.

Om's mother had been working with the other women in the neighbourhood ever since she was ten years old. The life of a *bidi* worker was relentless and unforgiving. To make a thousand *bidis* a day, one would have to start from six in the morning and go on for a few hours after midnight. Trammelled in their saris, they perspired all the sweat their bodies could hold only to make sure that their families did not famish. Every second of their lives expired through the smokestack of this struggle, quietly waiting for their lungs to stop breathing one day. There was no day, no night and no spring.

But the miracle of this woman, which was also defining characteristic of every man, woman and child in the neighbourhood, was that despite all the manifest cruelty that chronic shortage of work, disease, deaths and debts had levied, she had managed to remain completely human and to persist throughout her life clinging only onto her deeply-sowed values and beliefs. People in this neighbourhood helped the weak, adopted the orphaned and nursed the sick, the lepers and the untouchables. It was incredible how they were united into a community that put love and mutual support into practice, that was tolerant of all people, and sacrificed for neighbours and even strangers.

Om's mother had put the chops onto the stove. She kept the food in little containers made of newspapers, I observed. Perhaps, she bought food in very minute quantities, so there were no actual containers or jars.

I tried to fiddle with the *bidis* that lay on the floor. It took me nearly fifteen minutes to prepare one *bidi* for every time I tried to tie the knots of silk, the whole thing would come off. The mother and the son laughed several times at my utter lack of grip. It would perhaps take me a whole lifetime to make 1000 *bidis*, I thought. And to think that from the age of six this little boy has been doing this work made me feel embarrassed. The very nature of this work that he was bracing himself for seemed to me to become progressively more monstrous with time, but his tireless little brown hands and the unflagging concentration in his eyes were not willing to yield. Within seconds, the *bidis* began to pile up on the old newspaper.

The rice and the dahl were ready. It was enough for only two people. Their mother ate only once, at night. Om himself would not eat anymore in the afternoon because he had come with a full stomach from school. I was given a full plate. I refused several times, but it fell on deaf ears.

"Sir, you won't be able to do this. This kind of work is not for people like you," she said as I ate. "The most time-consuming part is cutting the papers to the right size because if the size is not correct, then the company will reject the lot. When we finish making the *bidis*, we collect them together and go to the company's ware-house. After selecting the lots, the company only puts the labels along with the packets and then sells them."

Om was an insightful young boy. He possessed a sharp and incisive but untended intelligence and aptitude towards math, developed from forces of frugality playing in his life. He could calculate in his mind the exact differences and products of numbers at an oracular speed which, I assumed, he had acquired from the family dealings with traders. Smartness and inquisitiveness ran in his veins and he could pick up things by sheer eyesight. As I often read his assignments, I found them outstanding, neat and precise-much like his *bidi*-making. I often praised his assignments in class, lauding him and holding it up as an example for other students, hoping that he and everybody else would continue to work more diligently on my assignments. But he never took interest in my congratulatory and supporting words. Perhaps, years of neglect and desuetude that had metastasized though his mind had forced him to believe that he was unfit for education, that it was better to put his hands into this kind of labour. He knew that and it made him thoroughly feel the weight of the responsibility that had been imposed on him early on in life. He had assumed that he must always be sedulously busy: he had an utter distaste for things that other boys of his age would love to do and therefore he had no time at all to spare for those sorts of things. He would never be seen fighting in the streets or playing cricket for he had mentally prepared himself to fight for the family's membership into the city's growing economic class by working twice as hard as the rest of the neighbourhood's boys. The seriousness of the work of his life had made him so disciplined and industrious that I only wished in my heart that he had shown the same dedication towards school.

"Sir, do you think making *bidis* is a respectable job?" Om suddenly asked me, without looking at me in the eye.

Only a day before in the class, I had taught the noun 'respect' and its corresponding adjective form 'respectable'. I did not know why he asked me that, but his sententious remark had immediately pushed me into the most unplumbed trenches of sadness. I would have liked to believe that if he could work harder at his studies he would not fail; but sitting in that room, one could feel that life had never respired in the freshness of that universal hope. He knew however that he was a beast of burden born for this kind of intensive labour, almost like a mule.

The most distressful part of this inhuman venture of their lives was not the physical hardship and clear hierarchy of near slavery, but the humiliation and the sad resignation that the verve of the human mind had been defeated and stewed to ashes long ago. As though, it was not his job to understand science and appreciate the beauty of literature and perhaps no one really cared if he could make those finer judgements. For his judgements, he had begun to depend on me because he thought I knew everything in the world about what was right and wrong, good and bad.

Om lifted his head from his work, while his hands were still at it, and looked at me quickly for once. He forced his lips to give me a dry smile and then returned his eyes to the *bidis*. I knew from his stare that he was not waiting for my reply. He had somehow figured it out. I believe circumstances had taught him that the mere goodness or badness of things did not matter in a life of utter irrelevance. What sense would he possibly make of a world where adult interests doused his dreams?

I was left completely discombobulated by his question. As a knee-jerk reaction, I tried to imagine him like that but I couldn't. I did not know where to find an answer. It hung around me like the dust clouds of tobacco in the room that were dry-heaving his breath.

I have never been able to answer him. And every time I have shared Om's story with my colleagues, I have not been able to hold back my tears. His words still linger around me and whenever its vibrations from that pulseless room resound in my ears, I sit motionless with a receding heart thinking how his life would slowly burn out like one of the million *bidis* he made and settle under the feet of men like a flimsy layer of dust. It was unbearable to imagine that one's whole existence could be described in that simple but clear question that had no answer.

There are times in our life when the pursuit of truth and real purpose acquires a profound significance that it rewrites the laws of the world in which we live. Its thrust is so powerful that it cannot be accurately captured in this spare narrative. For me, that moment had come.

Through the thin filament of Om's heart, I had looked into the bottomless pit of this suffering neighbourhood where generations of children are caught in a perpetual cycle of hope and failure. Yet there are times when the friction between infatuation and disenchantment melts in the light of a promise that shines over the surface of their very being. If one looked through the mirror of their hearts, one could see on it a simple vision of a good meritorious life where one lives with moral certainty and self-respect. That was their heaven of freedom, their springtime.

ELEVEN

In a school that was as small as ours and with only a handful of teachers, it was very common for a teacher to know about a good number of students even without the existence of a formal student-teacher relationship. Hedi was one such student. He was in the seventh standard of the Urdu-medium and he went by the name of Captain. He was a big able-bodied *man* with a large sun-burned face and long powerful arms. His head was shaven and his eyes were reddish-yellow and seated deep inside their sockets; they seemed to look beyond the spectator. His chin was sunken into his face like a deflated balloon and it was covered with a thin layer of beard that spread below the floor of his jaws. Yet his whole countenance was written with ferocity. As if he was made of granite. He was nearly seventeen years of age; therefore he was much older than the rest of the students. He had failed several times during the previous academic years and yet he came back to school every year, even if it meant to study in the same classroom.

To the other children, he was like an ogre who had jumped straight out of their nightmares. They were mortally afraid of him for he led the secret gangs of the school.

This gang included some of the most notorious boys from the Marathi-medium as well. They were responsible for paralyzing the school's law and order situation and wreaking havoc almost at the drop of a hat. Most of the beatings and fighting that had happened in the school were circumstantially connected to them. In addition to the existing code of discipline in the school, they had proposed their own set of rules that all the students had to obey if they had to survive in the school.

The first time I had met him was on the day when I was substituting in their classroom for their math teacher. This was because the headmistress of the Urdu-medium section had requested me to since there was no teacher competent enough to teach them that subject. At first I thought I would refuse. I did not wish to take on an added responsibility over and above my original students, but prudence and discretion guided me otherwise.

Hedi was twenty minutes late but did not bother to ask for permission before entering. He pushed the heavy door aside, barrelled in and sat at the end of the classroom with two other students, who looked like his sidekicks. Three buttons of his shirt were open and the collar was raised like the ears of a dog. He looked rather weird in his old worn-out half pants, for it seemed as if the pants were bought when he was smaller in size and had not been replaced since. He did not have school shoes, he wore a dust-covered chappal that made a slapping noise as he walked down the aisle.

Through the entire class, he paid absolutely no attention to the lesson but kept chatting loudly enough to overtake me and making lewd comments at the girls, perhaps intentionally to demonstrate my weakness. I was reluctant to talk to him for I anticipated that his reaction might disintegrate the classroom. When I was finished, he walked out of the class with his friends ahead of me, shaking his broad shoulders and giving me the feeling that his sharp teeth was gnawing with mistrust and retribution.

I took another class in the same week and I realized that his propaganda was to ensure that those who wanted to study in class could not. He started off by denting, with pieces of brick that he collected from the field, all the furniture that he saw in the classroom. He got nearly three hours every day when he had no work to do. He utilised this time to rip planks off the desks and wrote abuses all over the walls. No disciplinary action worked with him; the teachers knew about the wide range of nefarious schemes and activities that interested him, but they were themselves scared. The class teacher of this class had herself asked me to avoid talking to him.

"We all come from good families, we are educated people. Why should we argue with these roughnecks from the slums and loose our own self-esteem? They are all devils from inside. They all look innocent, but stay with them for a while and see what shit they are made of. Talk of Hedi- that boy is the kingpin of devilry. We should hand him over to the *policewallas*, but we can't."

I thought I should discuss his case directly with the headmistress but even she spoke to me in a voice that had with the same degree of helplessness that I was experiencing, "There is just nothing I can do about this boy. I don't know why he even comes to school. Leave him alone for your own good."

Their gatherings happened on the roof of the school which was accessible only through an old staircase led by a passage from the back. The roof of the school had not been put to any use and consequently no one ever went in that direction. A collapsible gate had been put there many years ago after the local police had asked the school authorities to install the gate so that that no one from the outside could reach the roof.

Two weeks after I had been to Hedi's class, Juneid, a student in my own class, had cut my lesson with the excuse of a toilet break and had not returned for half an hour. The rest of the students were getting restless and creating more noises than the usual about his not coming back. I decided to send one boy to look for him. He came back panting and said, "Sir, I have looked everywhere, he is nowhere in the school." That was not possible. Juneid was not one of those boys who dared to escape from school. Almost instantly, I was fogged by the fear that he might have been beaten up somewhere and he was unable to come back.

I gave an assignment to the class and went out looking for him myself. I searched the area near the toilet, walked along the back wall, and checked the hall-room. He was really missing. Then like lightning it struck me. Could he have gone towards the roof, I thought? Hardly had the thought come to my mind when I dashed towards the passage in the direction of the roof.

Before this day, I hadn't come to this part of the building. There was no one in the passage or the staircase, only rubbish was lying there. The whole place smelled off pungent chemicals and adhesives. Upon reaching the roof, I found the gate had been left open. Someone had broken the lock. It must have been done long ago. I pulled the gate a little aside and came to the roof.

Hedi was sitting in the center with his two sidekicks and one boy whom I instantly recognized as the student from the Marathi-medium who had brutally beaten up a little boy from third standard in the toilet a few weeks ago. The other member in the circle was Juneid who was shuffling a deck of cards. They were rolling up cigarettes and passing the joints over to the others. One of his sidekicks held a bundle of ten and fifty rupee notes.

It took a few seconds for the students to notice that I was standing. But I was all too shocked myself to see such a spectacle in the school. I did not know what to tell them. I did not want to try them either. I knew that I was palpably at a disadvantage against those boys who were physically stronger than I was. Besides, there was no point in pulling them by their collar and getting them another suspension for those little punishments would have made no difference. His brother, as the teachers and *sevikas* have told and retold me, who had taken over the drug racket from their father and uncle was a regular face in the neighbourhood's police station.

Not a word was exchanged between them and me. I only kept looking at them with stern eyes while they filed out of the roof one by one. Their chappals biffed like soldiers on a drill, on their way down. He left in the end, after putting the lighter and the crumpled cigarettes back in his pockets.

The bangarang that followed the shadows of Hedi and his friends did not necessarily decline after this incident, but he had suddenly begun to show a certain degree of deference towards me. To be respected by a boy so thoroughgoing in his notoriety seemed rare and strange to me. At first I thought that it was one of those usual pretensions that children show to win favours from teachers. He knew very well that no teacher in the school, not even me, could literally exercise any real authority over his gang, yet a vague semblance of rapport began to emerge. Perhaps this was the first time he had shown any sign of respect to someone in the school, I thought. Whenever I would pass by their gang, I would hear him mumble, "Keep quiet". They would immediately keep their heads down and refrain from using slang language for a while like perfectly obedient children until I went far. He also started coming up to me with a lot of things only to start a conversation. He would begin with a greeting "Sir, how are you? How are your students?" "What are doing this year in sports?" This felt good.

In the weeks that followed, we interacted more like friends than as a teacher and a student. I looked upon him like any other boy in the school and not a menace. His misbehaviour lessened significantly although he was still very volatile and sensitive. The other members of his gang also began to surround me as soon as they had realized that I did not intend to have a confrontation with them.

From them I had learned of the history of gang violence in the school. Fury that often originated somewhere in the slums meandered its way into the school and was settled eventually in the school's toilets or rooftop. And often insignificant trifling incidents of fighting over each other's possessions turned into vehement face-offs. But the situation had aggravated when about six years ago a boy in the English-medium school was forcefully beaten up by a bunch of boys from the Urdu-medium for not repaying money he had borrowed from them. The twelve year-old victim was lifted up on all fours by the gang members, tied with ropes and put inside an empty rice sac and kicked. This incident was followed by another brutal incident that took place outside the school when a boy had driven a knife through a girl's hand because the girl had denied him from having a physical intercourse with her. Both these incidents had caused children and parents alike in the two schools to lose faith in the administration's ability to contain violence. And as the teachers of the two schools pointed fingers at each other, the gangs of the English-medium had soon sprung up to curb the omnipotence of the boys from the Urdu-medium.

But although we were on good terms now, it was hard to get Hedi to come to my class. I knew why and I did not force him to be present. When only two weeks were left for the first-terminal examination, I caught him during the break. His eyes were red and his legs were tottering unsteadily. He was high on weed. I held his hand firmly so that he would not fall and told him that if he continued like this, he would fail. He shook his hand off me and left. Then one day later, he appeared at the door almost in the middle of my class. He said he was sorry for having missed several of my classes asked if I would let him enter. He spoke with so much friendliness as if he was talking to his own brother that I allowed him gladly. During the class however, he stayed mostly to himself, appearing not to be interested in what was going on.

After the first class he attended, he started being present in almost every class, ignoring others while the lesson was on. He would not look at me or at the charts on the board but his ears would be straight up. Words came out of him, but only in small instalments. After a few classes, he came up with doubts, asking me to explain further after class with easier examples.

Hedi's growing interest had surprised students and teachers alike. Some of them believed that something about his attitude had changed, others still thought it was his usual slyness and that he had something dangerous back in his mind that I should be mindful of. When I asked him, he said, "I can't be sitting here in a classroom all my life. I need to finish what I started."

Over the next few weeks, I earned the opportunity to teach him a few basic concepts of math after the usual hours of school got over and I realized that he possessed, like many other students in my classroom, some of the natural intelligence and aptitude that had been nearly thoroughly despoiled by severe lack of practice and encouragement. He had tremendous instincts and a real passion for problem solving. It took only a matter of seconds to go down to the root of a problem. He did not need to memorize the lessons from the books.

My initial frustration with him got over as he began to see the sincerity of my friendship and I made an almost unshakable commitment to make this boy succeed in school. I found time out of my tight schedule every day to make sure that he was well prepared for the upcoming tests. I gave him as much material- notes, assessments and question banks- as I could and asked him to practice them at home. I knew it was a lot of work and he might not bother to finish.

Astonishingly he had completed most of these assignments in a matter of just two days.

Yet with a boy like him, I had to tread gently with him for I knew the odds of losing him again were high. One day, he allowed me a free pass into his soul. I accepted the invitation and visited his home in the slum a few evenings later.

The neighbourhood in which he lived can be described, by all means, as dangerous. It had a reputation so terrible that even the auto rickshaw drivers refused to take me there. The neighbourhood housed the families of local gang members, convicts, prisoners and outlaws. The mafias and slum lords who lived right across the slum controlled most of the activities of the slum, which ranged from eviction of families for non-payment of rent, earning money from distributions of drugs, dens of alcohol to black marketing and control of political activities.

The precincts of the place had the look of a devastated shantytown. From the thick population of tenements, I guessed the slum must have had a thousand homes, low-level huts with roofs made of brick tiles or thin sheets of tin and covered with plastic bags. On the main road that led to the slum inside, there were a good number of industrial premises alongside a tannery, a chemical factory and a mill which did their best to provide livelihood to the families of the slums.

As I crossed the train tracks around which the bulk of inhabitants of this neighbourhood settled, my mind tried to find its feet in the alternative reality I was stepping into. I crossed through little awnings and cracks in the walls, along the arterial gutter that ran through the slum like a bloodline. Choked with plastic, it has become a parallel track to the narrow dirt road. Everything here bespoke the abject poverty and despair of the place that left me gasping. It seemed to fit perfectly into the way a slum is defined under Maharashtra's laws- a congested, unhygienic area or as buildings that are public hazards. But none of the other settlements in the Peth that I had visited had such deep lines of desperation written over them. It was as if this do-or-die quality of life was an acceptable feature of this slum. I made my way into this ant colony through a jumble of narrow lanes, stinking from the smell of refuse that had not been cleaned from the drains for perhaps a month. People who lived could not have been normal, I thought to myself, because normal people wouldn't be able to walk around with a clear conscience with so much dirtiness suppurating about them.

I asked an old woman if she knew of Hedi. She reached her shaking hand out in the direction of a series of small tenements with a few trees covering them. A narrow winding path among the trees led to a pool behind the front part of the slums and the other tenements stood around the pool. This was a pool of dirty water, mud and excrement.

I found him sitting in the porch made from dry mud. He walked up to me and welcomed me inside. It was a one-roomed hut made mostly out of sheets of tin. It had a cot in the left end and two windows which had iron rods attached. A chest of drawers was placed on the floor near a chair with a crippled leg. The wall was decorated with aluminium utensils-several small pans, a spatula, a whole spoon, a slotted spoon, meat chopper and a few plates, bowls and cauldrons- hanging from hooks. I sat on a partly broken chair and observed the place.

As little remnants of sunlight began to disappear, I became more aware of the echoes of life happening around the house. A swarm of mosquitoes from pool had just begun to wake up from their sleep to infect the people of the neighbourhood. These mosquitoes would not let anyone sit at one place for more than a minute. People from the neighbourhood started gathering around the house. They smoked, drank and talked boisterously. Gambling games started in isolated places. People put their money up. Some put up other things like rings from their fingers.

Hedi was very happy that I had found the time to come to his place. It was the usual business time for the family and customers were coming and going. He sold packets of weed for 40, 60 and 100 rupees. There was a younger boy working with him, who would fetch the packets from the lower drawer of the chest. He was his uncle's son.

"My father and uncle are in jail," he told me. "It is very tough to live here. We are, after all, illegal residents. The pradhan controls everybody's lives. We have to abide by what the pradhan says, like puppets. But the pradhan's men won't let us do business here. They come all the time to threaten my mother. They are looking for Alam, my elder brother. He is hiding because he fell out with one of their gang-men over a deal three months back. Since then, their men are looking for him. He is living in secret storehouses and brothels." While he spoke, he took puffs from a smoking pot kept behind him.

His father had a heart attack in jail but they can't go to see him there.

"Oh they will pick me up and beat me to death. I will show you how they beat me the last time the two police officers came here asking me for my brother. I did not scream. I did not yield."

When he said that, there was a visible sense of pride in his voice. There were no pretensions in what he said and I could understand the sentimentality that was perhaps peculiar to his kind of people.

In a way, his world was a world apart from everyone else's, living apart from the world. To understand his world, one would have to put down all known notions of rationality and idealism. One cannot compare him beside people like us; one would have to compare him to the adolescent boy in next door who had seen the mafia lords beat his mother and rape his sister. Given the anonymity and horror of his life, I was amazed how he could afford to come to school.

His mother arrived soon after the evening fell. The neighbourhood was now lit up by a handful of bulbs and tube-lights. She came with a stainless steel plate in her hand which held a coconut and a small lamp. She had come from the mosque.

"Who is he?" she asked Hedi in a dull gross voice of listless despair. "My teacher," he replied with an inflated chest.

He told me that she had just returned from Alam's place, her elder son. No one knew about his identity and his whereabouts except for the family. Even they were unsure if he would ever return to the slum, she said. But whatever else was unsure in this fetid dunghill of a world, a mother's love was not. It was the only thing real, pure and untarnished.

The hoodlums had also threatened him and beaten him a few times on his way to school. They beat him out of anger because they could not catch his brother. Hedi also did not go without a fight, he said. As he told various stories from his life, I felt something rare. It was how two people from two different worlds found themselves linked by a bond of sympathy, like an elder brother and his younger one, who owed nothing to the rules and expectations of others.

It was late night, probably nine o'clock, when I got up to leave. But as I walked away from his house one question kept the discomfort welling inside me: how could education ever be possible in such a place where hordes of unlucky children like him were lost in the labyrinth of utter wretchedness and destitution. Yet, and I don't know why, the more he troubled me, the less I could forget him; and the more I learned about his condition, the less I wanted to leave him alone. But he had struck me with an even deeper concern: What did education really mean to him? What difference could it make in the chances he had in his life? In this reckless turmoil of adults, children and animals, knowledge was like an empty bottle. One would only have to hope for eye-blinding miracles to take place if one ever had to educate these children. But miracles like that don't happen easily inside a hovel.

My assignment to teach the Urdu-medium class had ended soon after the examination was over. Many of the students had done well and many had not. Hedi had managed to pass with a little leniency from my side. I began to devote most of my time to my own seventh grade students again. But for a few weeks Hedi went missing from school. I checked all of his usual locations but they were empty and I ended up spending more time with the boys in his gang, hoping to elicit some information about him.

These boys also liked the time they got to spend with me, probably because I was the youngest of all the male teachers in the school and they could talk with a lot more ease and comfort with me. The boys and I had in common a passion for sports and sports cars. They never stopped talking of the Indian Premiere League, of the teams they supported and of batsmen and bowlers. They told me when and where they had spotted an expensive sports car speeding by. They had no idea about Hedi however. One of his sidekicks was Haseeb, who lived very close to his hut. Only he informed me that that the door of their house was locked. The mafia's men had shut down their business.

The prolonged absence of a student was not an uncommon thing in our school but by the time the absent students came back, their attention and interest towards school would have crepitated and it would get even harder to cover the loss. In Hedi's case, my worries were more serious. I wanted to find out why he was not coming to school with the urgency and concern of an elder brother. I did not bother so much about his progress in class as I did for his safety. I had seen the face of danger snarling at him when I had visited him: Was he being pursued by the strongmen in his slum? What he being hunted by the police? Had he shot anyone or been shot? Sitting in a schoolroom, one could not find these answers.

I spent many sleepless nights brooding over him. I couldn't get him out of my head. I still can't get him out. I spent hours thinking about his situation that to my mind defied the known laws of possibility and these thoughts continued to haunt my mind every day and night when he was not there. Anyone who had ever got close to him would have sensed his impending demise from a long distance. Even he knew of it very well but he would keep it away with brave words. That way he thought he could win over his fears. "Nothing will ever happen to me," he had assured me, "You will see, sir, that one day I will come out all this very safely. Things will get worse and then they will get better."

It was in the middle of spring when I saw him come back to school. He had come back after about eleven weeks. During this time, he had grown a little taller. He looked older than before but thinner now. His bones had protruded and cracks had started to appear all over his face. He appeared very sick inside. He looked at me cursively as I passed him hurrying off to a staff meeting. I had no time to greet him but I felt contended to see him back.

I met him again in the break. He was standing among his gang near the toilet, one of their old stamping grounds. This time, I went up to him. As always before, I could smell the smoke of cigarette and weed as I came close to him. I asked him how he has doing. But he ignored and walked away from me.

At first, I thought that his stone-cold rigidity might have come from his long respite from school but as the week passed, it became clear to me that he was really struggling with himself. His eyebrows were always bent, his face covered and lost in thoughts. He had stopped talking to me completely and spent his time smoking or loitering all over the place.

Over the next two weeks, his appearance changed to that of a madman. His body become dry and his face, which had become very dark, carried pockmarks like the ones seen in people who suffer from pox. He had lost all his strength and ferocity. A faint glimmer of fear had begun to pierce the fog of his mind. Even from a long distance, his eyes told me that his end was unstoppable and he was swallowed in the very contemplation of it.

That day was Hedi's last in school. One would have never imagined that boy of his kind would disappear before our eyes without leaving a trace. I never realized what had happened to him until his chum Haseeb threw light into his disappearance. He told me that the mafia of their slum was bent on terminating the family since the night his elder brother had killed the mafia's nephew on a highway. His brother had been hunted down and killed. Hedi knew that he would be the next. He knew that he had no chance anymore. He had put all his stakes to turn life in his favour and failed. His only way was to flee with his mother.

Hedi fitted only in the gutters and sewers of the world which had failed him. Naturally, no one in the school cared to find out about him or spare a thought for him. I was not surprised when not even one teacher regretted that he was untraceable. Throughout the time I knew him, the teachers had only questioned his ability to acquire strong values and good qualities, but never his eagerness to change himself. But whose values are we really talking about?

Hedi left no ripples in the water, no footprints in the sand, except for a few close friends who had now begun to doubt the chances of their own survival. But such stories were not happening in their lives for the first time. In life's battle, they were soldiers giving themselves up one after another. Those who survived had very little power to control their fearful imaginations and visions of seeing others perish or fade into the unknown, but by the time they grew up they would have learned to ignore the days of horror with a shrug and pretend that it did not matter who lived and who left them.

It is easy for one to keep a safe distance from boys like him and easier still to say that these slum children do not have a soul. But that is far from the truth. For boys like Hedi, who would be perpetually suspended between guilt and innocence, still try to smile every day pretending that in that way they will be able to overcome their looming fears. In every little word and action of this flailing teenager, I was a witness to the interminable willingness in him to be good and virtuous. He was trying always to stop hating himself and to forgive society for casting a glare at his family. The weed he took often made that magic happen easily by taking him out of the slum that looked like a prison into the disappearing unknown. But the magic lasted only hours and when he would regain his senses, all the pressures of the world would be slapping his back until he would fall unconscious.

Hedi's only weapons were his words- small, silent but consecrating. His words still rustle in my ears like a prayer that came from the innermost ring of his self-belief. Among them, there was one that I remember most.

"I want to leave all this shit one day," he had confessed to me with a long-drawn sigh, "and do some ordinary work like driving or shop-keeping. I want to work very hard. I don't want to be a *goonde* in this slum. I want to lead a good life and die a good death."

When he said that, I had thought that this boy really had no ambition in life. It had profoundly broken my heart that he did not want to aspire for more. While he did not want to be an outright criminal, his dreams were at the most an ordinary attempt to escape his life's situations. Most other boys of his age and providence would have dreams more far-stretched than him.

But as I kept thinking over his words through the rest of the night and for many weeks afterwards, I had arrived at a certain degree of clarity. Why did he choose to move? What made him uproot everything he had known for an unknown path? The answer is but a very simple one: he wanted to be better than what he was made of....he wanted to be recognized as better than the slum in which he lived. All people, including me, move in the hope of a better life. But what did a better life mean to Hedi? I imagined it would be a place where he would not wake up to the sound of a gunshot, a place where his hopes would not be left to the sounds of fierce winds, a place where the infinite sky glows with the brightness of being alive. He tried to warm his perishing joy in that glow, transmuting his daily experiences into the radiance of an everlasting life. For a boy like Hedi, to dream was to fill up that ever-widening empty space of his world that was created many years ago when he had seen love and childhood die. It was not an ordinary dream for all his life he was constantly trying to change his world to resemble the faint image of that world he dreamt of. In every breath and every thought, he had renewed his hope and longed to go there. When he was gone, I knew inside he had found what he was looking for.

TWELVE

It had taken five months for the teacher who taught the sixth standard students to return to school. This teacher, 25 year old Ms Kedal, had originally joined the school in the last academic year; however since the beginning of this year, she had been on leave and while Mrs Khan had been promising me every month that she would return, she never did. During her long absence, the general pandemonium in this classroom had almost absolutely prevented me from teaching lessons without losing my focus.

The fate of the children in this classroom had become a seed of profound distress for me. There were only thirty students in the sixth standard. In the previous year, there were twenty more children in the class who dropped out of school at the end of the academic year. And some simply left.

Knowledge had for long settled in the bottom of a deep pond dug in the middle of this teacher-less classroom. The school administration had been unable to assign a teacher with any decent qualification and competence for three long years. These decisions were made by the *Education Board* and the school had no say in them. Last year, a female teacher had been teaching this class for three months but she could never reach school on time. She stayed with her family in a village near Baramati. It was about four hours from Pune by bus. Till then, the children were left to their own machinations. After two months, this teacher got married and immediately applied to the Zila Parishad to get recruited in a school in Baramati. In the meanwhile, the children had moved another step further in the direction of absolute vehemence and perversion.

It was natural that under the constant influence of such a discouraging environment, the children became more and more dispirited. They frequently resorted to combats, abuses and the flirtatious company of girls to keep themselves busy throughout the day. When the school administration finally took notice of the gravity of the situation, they suggested that I should take up responsibility for the classes.

Although she was already 25, Mrs Kedal was still in her third year of college. She had not graduated yet. She had joined the government teacher training institute in her first year of college and earned her diploma in two years. While she taught in the school, she was also preparing to retake her college examinations.

Teaching in the same din and bustle of the classroom, Ms Kedal and I soon became very good friends. Ms Kedal possessed an amicable and empathising nature and unlike the other teachers, she did not deliberately maintain her distance with me. However, as I had anticipated, the obvious professional difficulties of co-teaching soon become apparent. When she taught, the cacophony of voices became so high that I was forced to suspend my lessons and wait till things calmed down. Seeing that it was not working in my favour, I had to make a pact that when I would teach, her class would remain quiet. I would observe silence when her turn came.

Ms Kedal never taught in English but in Marathi. Consequently, her children had not made much progress in English either. "I went to Marathi-medium schools all through my life. As a girl, I used to take a bus to a good school in the town. It would take me three hours to get there. I wanted a good education," she told me. "No one ever encouraged me to learn English properly. That is why I cannot read well or write. I don't have any fluency. In my schooldays, when I tried to speak in English, my teachers and friends laughed at me.

"I could have got into better professions only if things had been different for me. Teaching is the only thing that I can do because I can't do or get into anything else. You have been able to do something with your lives because you had good teachers, good schools and your family to ensure that you make the most out of your opportunities. I never got that. I wanted to sit for the public service examinations like IAS and IPS when I was in high school. But that did not happen. My father had cancer and he died before my dreams. And then a time came when even a cheque of three thousand rupees at the end of every month became priceless in a family with no one to earn the bread. My mother had to support two other girls who were still in school. So I joined the teacher college, hoping that I will get this job quickly."

She lived in a dormitory with nine other women, all of whom had migrated from different small towns and villages and paid a third of her salary as rent. She tried to fiercely save every morsel of her salary so that at the end of the month, she could send it home. It seemed almost impossible to me how she managed to do this.

"Our teacher training college is like a mega-factory to produce teachers. Those who come, they eat drink and spend their time well. The government has a qualifying examination that teachers have to sit for after they get their diplomas, but for two successive years they have not conducted the exam putting one and half thousand teachers without a job. I was among those who passed the exam three years ago but they didn't put me in any school then. For a year, I sat without any job, without any pay. Then they said they want four lakhs. That's the *rate* here. If you had a rank in the exam, then they can make some concessions. You don't have a choice in these matters. The whole system is designed to run like that. But once you can get into a school, you are safe. No one would touch you anymore."

This was true of all the teachers, she believed.

"Mr Gaikwad used to collect money every year from the students' parents promising them to make their children pass in the final examinations. He is saving it for his promotion."

In addition to her mounting financial stress, Ms Kedal had a perceptible disadvantage that became a source of anxiety and fear. Being quite young in age, she had become an easy target for the boys in the school. The more she tried to discipline them, the more they whistled and sang at her. The neighbourhood around the school which she had to pass through everyday was also not a merciful one. It being tainted with all kinds of attacks and harassment upon women had forced her to stay away from school.

"You don't know Sir," she told me, "What I have gone through with these children last year. They abused me all the time from underneath their noses. The moment I turned away from them, slangs were thrown at me. Can you call them innocent? Javed and his brother Riaz come from a family that looks after the auto-rickshaw unions here in their area. They threatened me by taking out a blade. You wouldn't know what I felt like every time when their fathers cast provocative glances at me. It was impossible to teach in this school. I had asked for a transfer after the year had ended and then I waited all these five months but the people at the *Education Board* rejected my application. They asked me to pay another one lakh rupees if they wanted my case to be considered. Where will I get that much money?"

There was a perceptible jot of anger and concern in her tone, as if the insults to her dignity had enervated her inner belief and acceptance of her children. She had given up hoping for things get better for her. Yet despite that, I began to appreciate her for how she was still ready to come and teach with a firm commitment and a formidable courage that would be the envy of any teacher.

After a few weeks, I had however convinced Ms Kedal that we should plan and organise classes for the teachers to help them improve their English grammar and writing skills. After cajoling Mrs Khan for days, we successfully held one class in my classroom one afternoon after school got over. Four teachers participated. Ms Kedal and I taught one basic lesson in nouns. The class was mostly disturbed by a bunch of children who stood at the door laughing at their teachers who were reduced to students and the teachers shooing them away every time they came back, but otherwise it went fairly well. This was followed by another class on verbs, then adjectives, prepositions and sentences. The teachers found it fairly interesting to go back to the books again. "You keep on taking more classes," one of them said. "It will help us revise most of these old stuff. We would not have any difficulty in teaching them."

Our efforts however ended abruptly when in addition to school's present trials, in December, the *Education Board* had served a letter upon the school informing Mrs Khan that she had been suspended for manipulating the school's accounts and defalcating the school's funds for her own use. By the records, the school had five hundred odd children but Mrs Khan had shown the government that seven hundred children studied in the school. In place of ten teachers, she had shown fifteen and parked the grants in her pockets. When the government officers took an inspection of the school, Mrs Khan brought children from outside and put them in the classrooms. How had she managed to do all this was still a mystery. There were rumours in the school that her brother-in-law ran an NGO that was behind this manoeuvre.

Mrs Khan's departure however created a visible concern among the teachers about what could be its possible implications upon them. So far, the teachers had earned the leniency and goodwill of Mrs Khan so that they could get away with whatever they wanted. The masterful technique they used for this was outright persuasiveness and insincere compliments. Mrs Khan had a weakness for it. It made her feel a little more powerful in an otherwise small insignificant world. But, with her disposal on the way, speculation began as to who would be appointed in her place. These theories and surmises, often incomplete and unfounded, went to such an extent that they became the most crucial subject of debate in the school- it was there during assembly, after assembly, during class, during break, after the break and even continued after school, ceaselessly for two weeks or so. The multiplicity of the hypotheses that circulated among the school staff had affected Mrs Khan and blown her reputation into pieces. She had however made one last attempt to bend the strings of the *Education Board* under the faint hope that she might be able to reverse the decision. The *Education Board*'s order however was not malleable.

Before Mrs Khan left, a small parting ceremony was staged by the teachers and a few children whom she had taught for a while. The new person in charge of the school was Mrs Chandane. She had been teaching in a school in Katraj for more than fifteen years. Mrs Chandane was as calm as the summer sea and quite pleasant to talk with. But, as it turned out very soon, her outward calmness and equanimity concealed the image of a doctrinaire monomaniac, ruthless in soul and pitiless in action, who openly gave us the freedom to apply brute force on children whenever needed.

Although many teachers were in the habit of practising the tradition of corporal punishment every so often during Mrs Khan's time but now their acts were not only legitimatized, but also glorified and encouraged.

I don't know the how the use of terror, for purposes that are manifestly inhuman, should do in the sins in the minds the children. I argued against it a couple of times with her but she and the teachers now seemed to have assumed an authority to impose upon the children their prejudices, their contortions, as well their "higher social status", perhaps only to serve their vindictive purposes and a deeper ideological intention that these children never escaped the circle of oppression into which they were born. For the children however, adapting to this world was tougher than they thought.

The whippings were administered with meticulous rigour and Mrs Chandane seemed to be absolutely justified and "fair" in the corrective methods she applied on the wrongdoers. These cold-blooded executions happened routinely on the open field and as I watched from the top corridor, I teared up in one eye to see the children being agonized and insulted in this manner- all done in the name of their moral liberation.

One morning in January, when the mercury had dipped below 9 degrees, I saw Mr Ingale dragging a little boy towards the office. He held him by the neck. Mrs Chandane was standing with her cane. The victim was Lokesh. His elder sister, Mitali studied in my class and I had visited their hut in the Peth over half a dozen times. He was in the first standard and was generally a very placid boy with no memorable records of disruption.

I was watching the scene from a corner on the upper floor. The poor creature did not protest. He looked down at the floor stolidly because he felt mortified for being treated like that. He quivered with cold fear of what was about to happen. Mitali ran out of the class and stopped before me. "Wouldn't you do anything?" I closed her eyes.

Mrs Chandane had ordered Mr Ingale to bash him on the leg with the whip. He obeyed her order but Lokesh stood there motionlessly without any reaction. He was trying to bring together the maximum strength that his weak body could hold to withstand the impetus of the whip. After the first attempt to overthrow him failed, she asked him to hit again with a shift movement of her eye. This time the teacher, looking happier, socked the boy even harder at the same place. For a brief second, Lokesh shook up but quickly became firm again. I shook up at the same moment for it seemed to me that if she wished, she could continue with the beatings until the victim became unrecognizable. A few more shots were aimed at him and each time it happened, an impish smile arising from a much cherished pleasure of total domination glistened on the surface of Mr Ingale's lips. At last, he started crying out loud. He could not hold it any further. His scream resonated through the building with intense pain. I lowered my head in shame, unable to bear the spectacle anymore.

The incident with Lokesh reached every parent in the neighbourhood like wildfire but there was absolutely nothing they could do. The parents knew both Mrs Khan and Mrs Chandane less than their children but the parents feared them more than their children did. And yet one would not believe that these were the same parents who would get into a terrible scrap, and even strike out, with their neighbours and other parents of the school if they said anything remotely hostile against their children. In the least, I had hoped that Lokesh's mother, who believed that her son was not guilty, would stand up for the boy. Instead she approached me. "We are scared of *Medam*. We cannot go and talk to her. If you could do something about this, then I could rest assured that my boy would not get beaten again."

I shared none of her reservations and decided to raise my concerns to Mrs Chandane first thing in the next week. I walked into the office and saw her standing with her back facing me. She was squalling at the *sevika* for being a delayer. But when she turned, my jaw dropped instantly and I bounced two steps behind her doorstep. Her face had been severely contused and the whole area around her right eye, which was closed, had inflated to double its size and become violet in colour. She looked like a chimera that had jumped out of my imagination. My throat felt dry, like a bone. I could not speak. She asked me if I wanted anything but I shook my head sideways and left the office in rapid steps. The inside of me had been shaken up so violently that it prevented me from conducting my lessons properly. A dozen times during the day, that face flashed before my eyes.

During the lunch break, I met Mrs Yasmin S. Unlike other days, she also appeared slightly disturbed, probably by the luridness of the incidents happening in the school. I kept quiet trying to read her thoughts. "Have you seen Madam today?" she asked, meditating over her words. I nodded slowly.

"It happens at least once or twice at the beginning or end of every month," Mrs S said. I understood what she meant by 'It'. "Her husband is widely known for it in the circuits of teachers and principals. He doesn't do any real work. He starts drinking from early morning and then in the evening, he goes to a street-side club and throws away all the money into *satta* and cards. Sometimes he works here and there in petty jobs and then spills his little cash into his addictions in a day or two. She is the one who runs their family. They have a son and a daughter who are both still very young. But they are not important to him. His liquor and gambling must be paid for first. And whenever she refuses to foot his excesses, she is punished like this.

It is depressing that no one says anything." Mrs S became pensive and fell silent again.

The hair on my arms had stood up. To see a wretched woman living within a fatal oppressor. To see a woman trying to domesticate the same reality that disheartened her every day. To see a woman, crushed and defenceless in the face of exploitation, concealing her anguish under the brisk mask of a stern school teacher. It was indeed hard to believe that her absolutism had become a necessity to keep her existing. If this was the reality in the life of an educated woman, what argument could we take for all the poor innocent girls in the slums? My mind started to wonder.

Two months later, when the municipal election was over, Mrs Chandane decided to leave. Rumours ran rife in the school that she was deserting her husband. She called all of us to her office.

"I will not be here anymore."

She took her reading glass off, rubbed them with a handkerchief and then wiped off the emerging drop of tear from the corner of her eyes. When she left, she smiled at me and said something that will be forever engraved in the slate of my memory, "Remember that you are here for only one cause: to teach your students, to love them like your own and do what is best for them. Nothing else matters."

THIRTEEN

The drawings of my children still remain in my heart as some of the fondest and out-of-sorts memories of my first year as a teacher. And it was here that I came across an absolute maven of the art. Rayya, mercurial but intuitive, was quietly immersed in creative dreams. In other words, all the characteristics of a fine artist were mingled in her. Her paintings were punctuated by a profound degree of sincerity and the rapidity of her strokes along with her sense of colours made it seem impossible to believe that she had touched the brush for the first time in life. She mostly drew about her childhood but mixed with elements of the fantastic, drawing from her imagination, interwoven into a magical fabric. Some of her other paintings were characterized by sobriety and sharp focus expressing an almost unsentimental, unemotional vision but also a spiritual relationship with the world of things.

Rayya was an indescribably quiet and unmalicious child. She did not make many friends and did not talk to the rest, preferring to live confined in her own spectrum of thoughts. It was as if they did not matter to her. To fulfil her share of the world's conversation, she talked to herself by mumbling when she was alone. That way, she was assured that she had not ceased to exist in the world. Her art was the only other way she expressed herself, all her thoughts and sentiments manifested through them. Yet at studies, one may never find a more diligent student. Within a year under my tutelage, her English reading had improved from 10 words a minute to nearly 24 words a minute. Significant changes had come in her essay writing and comprehension skills. Her grades were nearly among the top three of my class.

Rayya had spent her childhood under the supervision of her aunt in their village because her parents did not have enough money at the time of her birth to feed her. When she was seven, she was brought to the slums to be united with her biological mother. She now lived a life surrounded by sewage. At home, Rayya never got a moment to spare for her thoughts. There was simply a lot of work which was followed by even more work. This kind of work was harsher than the work she did in her village. There work and rest happened in the intermittent periods but here there was no respite. Naturally, she did not have any time for art. School was the only time when she could think freely and draw.

But however her world appeared on the outside, a lot of things happened daily that failed the boundaries of reason and relationship such as a bout of routine beatings of an incomprehensible extremity. On the first morning in March, she came to school with dark bruises all over her hands and legs and even on her neck. She was drenched in lilac which had formed long thick lines against her whitish skin with occasional circles of reddened wounds. At first I could not fathom the sight but then I went over to her, pulled her out from the class. She tried to set herself loose from me but failed. I tried to lift her face and make her talk, asking her caringly what had happened the night before. The corner of her lips was half-closed from her wounds. I felt a wheezing birr coming from her pale white countenance which immediately told me that she was experiencing intense pain all over her body. She could no longer put up with it.

She had lost her ability to talk. She tried to get away from me by looking outside from the corridor with fixed eyes, while I kept repeating the same question. Waters started to make her eyelashes a little heavier every time I prompted her. When I asked for the fourth time what had happened to her, she broke her silence and burst out in tears. She bluntly admitted that her father had walloped him with a belt for several consecutive nights after returning home drunk. As she spoke, her heavy breath oozed the anguish that had been accumulating inside her little soul for a long time. This was not just the anguish that one faces when one is in physical pain, but another kind- the one that slowly poisons the heart of a little girl to rot and decay. She rushed into me and held me with both arms.

"Please help me. They are going to beat me again," she blubbed. This was not an ordinary child crying but a child in despair. Her tear-streaked face was pressed into my body and her cries soaked my arms and shirt. My head shook from one side to another. My mind had lost its control. I could not think of anything. "They are going to beat me to death," she muttered again and again.

The state of cruelty that had disfigured this poor girl had left her in an impossible state. She could not sit in class and take lessons. I put her in the room adjoining the headmistress's office where she was laid down upon a table to rest. She went into a long slumber. After school, I tried to sound the other teachers about her but discovered that nobody wanted to show concern. They either pitied her for her condition or accused her straight out for lying about her family.

"*Jhoot bolti hain ladki*," one of them yelled at her. Then turning to me, she said condescendingly, "These girls are full of filth. *Aap iske baat pe maat jao.* It is their life, after all. Let them do whatever they want to: let them die, kill each other, or throw their children away."

I realized that the teachers were too insentient towards the girl's ill-fate to do anything to protect her and figured that the nostrum of Rayya's problem could only be found if I met her father or mother. I jumped up on my feet and went to look up the school's registers. My fingers rolled through the pages until I came across her name and noted down her address in a little notebook.

In the midst of a thickly crowded bazar in Budhwar Peth, a narrow alley stretched down from the main road that faces one of the most beatified temples in the town. At the core of this deep heart of the Peth, a haphazard bazaar had sprung up. Apparently "tourists" and wealthy people were common in these parts.

Further ahead lay the city's infamous brothel neighbourhood. The street narrows into a lane, dotted with shacks offering everything from a haircut to a beer. The streets inside it were narrow and filled with double-storeyed tenements on both sides and women and children were leaning onto the railings of their drooping wooden balconies to look down onto the streets from above. At the corners and entrances to the houses, prostitutes were standing, waiting. I wondered what the insides looked like. Some women sat on the dilapidated staircases and dusty porches and men were lining up near their doorsteps.

In the last one year, I passed through such neighbourhoods in the city that I had stopped thinking about them. Today, I felt uncomfortable and disgusted again. Although Rayya's house was not in these brothels, this way was the only way to reach her slum. The other point of entry to the slum was blocked by a garbage dumping ground. I kept walking straight, my heart palpitating very fast. At the end of the street, I took a turn into a much darker alley and started inspecting the houses.

The whole slum had as its address the Number 138. Inside, people were perhaps sought by their names or perhaps by the stories of their lives. I scurried inside like a threatened rat trying to keep my head below an exhibition of clothes that hung onto ropes in zigzag fashion. Hostile gazes of men and women and animals beset me as I walked through the hovels. My eyes were looking everywhere for the girl. Then, a teenage girl passed by me carrying a bucket of water. She was from our school. Upon asking her, she showed me the way to Rayya's room. I walked a few more yards and took another turn. The second room from the corner was hers.

On the outside three garrulous men were sitting with a bottle of liquor and drinking raucously, the miasma of alcohol filling the entire doorway. The moment they saw my face, their hearty conversation ceased as one of them stood up and stared at me. I introduced myself and told him that I was looking for Rayya's mother. This man was large and had a sternly built body. His face was dark and his cheeks were broken with spots and lines. He was wearing a vest with holes all over it and a lungi. He said he was her father. He was drunk like a fish. He kept me waiting outside until his scepticism went away and he let me inside the house.

Their house had only two rooms, one inside and one outside where I was standing. As soon as I stepped in, an unnatural smell struck me. It was not the smell of water colours or the smell of new books. Rather it resembled the stench of sewage water rising from the drains.

A large bed stood at the corner of the room and opposite to it was a TV set in which a Marathi channel was going on. Right beside the TV, there was a wall in which square shaped compartments had been dug out to keep utensils and food. Rayya's father asked me to sit inside and gave a shrill call to her mother. Then he staggered to the outside to join his drinking group. After about ten minutes, her mother walked through the door and came to the room outside. Rayya was nowhere to be seen.

She began with a philippic about her daughter and condemned her for being such a pain to their family. "One day, I will kill this haramzadi," she squealed. "She cannot give us any more trouble. Let me see today how she escapes from my hands." That was when I realized that her mother was high on alcohol herself. Her eyes were red like blood and she could not keep her focus as she talked. Her words were inconsistent and her attitude struck me a hard blow and threw me into an uneasy state of mind. She kept on talking about how bad her daughter was and how much she wished to get rid of her. She gave a relentless lecture on morality and poverty and how stuck they were in their present state of life.

In her hokum however she suddenly slipped something out that shook my whole body instantly.

"We can't feed this girl anymore. We don't have money. We must get rid of her right now. My husband and I want to get our girl married this year. Otherwise she would keep growing older until no one would take her as a bride. But this girl doesn't understand what is good for her. She wants to go to school, read and write and paint all the time- all foolish things. All this will not help her survive her life. I also got married at an early age, then why wouldn't she?"

Hearing a mother talk this way, my pulse had skipped a beat. Rayya was 12-years old but for her family, there was nothing that could possess them more than the obsession to get their daughter married off quickly. No matter how much I stretched my imagination, I could not accept this. The thought of my own sisters who were of her age crossed my mind. They would be studying in school when this poor girl would be serving her husband's family. Sitting there in their room, I felt so broken and confused that I could barely speak. What sense could one make of a world where such things happen to children?

Realizing the urgency of the situation, I called Rayya's father, Yusuf, to school a few days later. He came drunk. Mrs S and I sat with for an entire hour, explaining to him why the girl should be kept in school and not disposed in this way. I said I was ready to help the family by putting the girl to a good private school in the neighbourhood and finding sponsors to support her education.

After a few days, Rayya's father came back to me for help. He said in a soft and gentle voice that he wanted to talk to me privately. We stood outside the school and talked.

He said that his family was down at the heels and he had many loans to repay. The loans had accumulated to over thirty thousand rupees and nobody was willing to help him. If he failed to pay back, his auto rickshaw would be taken away. Given his straightened situation, he asked if he could borrow from me to fund his daughter's studies and promised in God's name to repay me within a month.

While I felt sorry for him, there was absolutely no way I could rely on his ability to repay. I tried to talk sense into him, but after a few minutes I realized that this man's desperation would not give way to my logic. I said I would help if I can, but promised him nothing. I contemplated for a few days, knowing that I could not expect money in return from this family. But at the same time, the fate of this poor girl kept haunting me. I worried that if nobody came forward to help, my student would meet the most unfortunate circumstances. After about two weeks time, within which Yusuf had come to me three times asking me again for help, I agreed to give him ten thousand rupees for her education.

I decided to visit their house again, two days later.

That evening, I led myself through the lights of the bazaar and the prostitutes again. But Rayya's house was locked and pieces of furniture stood outside, like skeletons. I searched for them frantically, knocking on people's doors and asking for them. Some could say nothing. Some said that they did not know what happened. One said that they had left this place. I stood there, flummoxed like a flight of dark shadows with a soul heavy-laden with trouble that will not depart. Could it be true? Could it have happened? I felt maddened. At that moment, and for the first time, I did not want to think of her anymore. I did not want to care for her anymore.

That night I spent in semidarkness. My whole body was rattling in fear and gloom. The night seemed longer than other nights. There was no electricity and I kept turning right and left. Sleep was hard to come by. I sunk down in consuming disappointment thinking how hard and reckless the reality was for a twelve year old to be entangled in a losing battle to save her childhood.

It would be hard to describe the intensity of this human drama.

Rayya had thudded me into complete silence. To those who loved her, she became a tormenting thought and her loss grew robust and alive. Her story never completed its circle like an unfinished work of art. Between the two of us, what was left was an incomplete friendship flailing in the air.

Her last memory was a painting that hung within a frame from the wall of my classroom. It was unspeakably unique. Its richness kept growing the longer one stared at it. It was a landscape of a wheat field put together from disjointed memories of her childhood in her village. The summer sun shone over the golden coloured sheaves of harvested wheat leaves gently bending over one another in the wind. A small girl in a vermillion skirt was standing and watching the fields with a sickle in her hand. She had reddish brown hair just like her. Her eyes were sad and joyous at the same time.

The wheat field had a deeper mystic significance for her. It carried in it the colour of dawn- a world full of the suggestiveness of her personality. It was not just a personal statement but a deep longing to unite with her childhood. Her whole world was ripe with the smell of wheat, ready for harvest. Staring at it had left me with a pervading feeling of disillusionment and angst that does not descend to the world, but rather only hides and palpitates behind it. My summer training at Teach For India had not prepared me for this day.

FOURTEEN

I thought that my voyage had come to its end
at the last limit of my power, that the path before
me was closed, that provisions were exhausted
and the time come to take shelter in a silent obscurity.
But I find that thy will knows no end in me.
And when old words die out on the tongue,
new melodies break forth from the heart;
and where the old tracks are lost,
new country is revealed with its wonders.

Tagore

It was the last poem I had taught my students. When I had read the poem myself, it had immediately struck a chord in my heart. To me, it signified the very reason why I had come to the city- to offer the generous gift of education to a community so needy of it, to break forth new paths where there were none and to rouse with new melodies souls weakened with loss. As I read the poem, I was reminded once again of the higher purpose of my work and the transcendence of education beyond the boundaries of race, class, religion, violence and vitriol. The vision of a new world had revealed itself to my eyes, perhaps the same vision that had inspired the poet many years ago, and immediately I knew from inside that my students would absolutely enjoy the poem's thought; they were the testimony of that great strength to conquer new worlds, the strength to aspire, to create and to believe in a better world. For nearly two weeks, I had wired my thoughts into how to best teach this poem, with many notes, carefully chosen examples and adjuncts to effectively convey its idea. However by the time I started teaching this poem, the context of our lives had changed forever.

In March, it became clear to me that many of them had silently made up their minds about ending school permanently. A few days passed since I had started explaining the theme of our poem when the quiet silence broke itself. First, it was Dana, the girl who above all had a deep interest in poems. When asked, she could explain a poem with such wide-eyed simplicity and perspicuously connect a poem to the real-world that many other students had begun to look forward to her interpretations.

Dana's mother was a tailor. She worked at a small loom and made about 4000 rupees a month. Her husband was an auto driver. The family was one of those many families that one would ordinarily find in these slums. There was nothing extraordinary about their circumstances. They were in a similar state of poorness like everyone else and fitted in the stereotype of hard-working people.

Dana's mother broke the news throwing a sudden sense of despair and helplessness at me. She had found work for her 14-year old daughter at a handloom factory run by a

Muslim businesswoman who lived in their neighbourhood. This woman who ran the loom belonged to the Momin group of the Muslim community and had risen to power in the neighbourhood due to her entrepreneurial skills. For the Momins, she was next only to god. She had put the poor Momins in the slum like Dana to work and ensured their survival, livelihood, health and protection.

Dana was being trained to weave clothes by the other women in the loom. Her friends told me that she was not sure if she could come to school anymore. I had not expected that Dana would end her school life so soon. My hopes for her were so high that it left me hanging with disappointment for many days. When I approached Dana's mother to bargain for her school days, she held the guns of her poverty to my head. She told me with both her hands joined together, "How will another year of education help her?"

"In our house," she went on explaining, "there is hardly any space to sleep properly, leave alone study. Our daughter will never be able to do with her books what other children do. Today or tomorrow she will have to go and find work. Making her study more is of no use then.

"A little extra money makes a lot of difference to us, sir. And our girl will learn some work also. Sahibjaan is a great woman. She is one of the oldest residents of the area. She has done so much for all the Ansaris in the slum. She got my husband an auto rickshaw to drive. The auto union leaders in this area don't always give the autos to Muslim people. But they respect her. We are grateful that she will give our girl a job. Don't worry about Dana. Allah's blessings are with her. She will do well."

Dana's face has disappeared from the pages of the school's musters into the hordes of child labourers working in the city. Work was always available at cheap rates for these children but what was disheartening was that children had no other choice they could pick from. Yet the one thing however had remained intact in her: her love for poetry. She had sent her friend Nazarene to ask me if she could borrow a book of poetry from my collection.

Dana was the first but not the only one to end her school-life so abruptly. By the third week of the unit, three more children from my classroom lunged into oblivion. Sohail was next. He came up to me and looked at me boldly. I thought he had come to request me for something that I would not grant.

"I am leaving this school next week."

I was confused and naturally I over-reacted. "Where are you going? You know we have got an examination coming up. If you miss anything now, you will not be able to cover up the loss."

"I am leaving school, sir. I am not going to come back here anymore."

The boy had made his decision. He would work with his father at their meat shop. He had already learned how to cut goats by working in the evenings at the shop. Now that the old man did not have enough blood flowing into his arms, Sohail had to steer the rudder for his ill-clad, ill-fed, louse-eaten family.

"Someone has to manage the shop. What shall we eat otherwise? How are we going to live?" he said. As the words fell out of his mouth, I realized that he was not complaining, nor was he asking for my approval. He was only telling me his decision.

Even though we're standing face to face in the same classroom, I left that we might quite easily be a thousand miles apart. I held his soft hands in my own and felt its texture. I was filled with pity. They were only twelve years old.

Like Sohail, Firoz was also leaving school before the year ended. I knew that he had given up on his education much before I had come and a mere graduation to secondary school did not matter to him. He had gambled his chances elsewhere. All the boys in his family had been sent to work after they turned fourteen. Firoz's uncle had got him work in a small hotel. He was getting paid two thousand a month for working at the kitchen. He wanted to start his own hotel once he had enough money.

"Look, I can't take this anymore. I want to make a lot of money in life. I want to be like one of those rich people. Who wants to live in a slum? I want to have my own house. I want to own a car someday. Those boys out there in our slum who are of my age are making good money already. Their pockets are full and they are happy. They get what they want. You will not understand, sir, what money means to people like us. We have very little of it so we need more of it."

In a slum, the influence of peers over the minds of these little boys and girls was often too strong to be defeated. I understood the perspectives in which he had been bought up all his life. I kept quiet. To him, all the poetry ever composed failed in the face of poverty. He could not anymore sit inside a classroom and see opportunities pass by. He had tried his hand but failed. Class seven was ending and he was just beginning to read and write correctly. Even a fool would be smart enough to guess that he had no business waiting any longer. It was better to drop out of school and pay for false papers to prove that he had reached the working age. And he did that.

"I don't like this torture of coming to school every day and sit in a classroom to become a donkey in life. I have done that for years and no matter how much you want me there, you don't know how hard our life is in the house. People in my slum tell me I am not good at anything and that I will have to go and work for those Hindu shopkeepers on the other side of our slum. I can't do that. I have got my own self-esteem."

His throat was dangling with a sense of hurt and confusion. As he spoke to me, I realized how terrified he must have been when he confronted the world's opinion of his apparent uselessness. He did not want to be denied what he thought was his. He did not want to be trampled under the feet of the power of the rich. For him the only way to make the world look him in the eye was by making a lot of money.

The other girl who had convinced me to believe that things in her life had changed for the better was Purva. She started working at a photography studio after school. Every time I had visited her house, she would be found washing utensils or dirty clothes at the public tap where the water came only in jerks for a certain time of the day.

On seeing me, she used to rub the sweat off her forehead and run inside her hut to call her mother. Her mother was a fragile and unsteady woman who had been weakened by several pregnancies and miscarriages. Despite her feeble health she always held out a smile for me. She would be acknowledging several times, to my utter embarrassment, that I was the right kind of teacher Purva needed. I would have never guessed by her enthusiasm and candour that she would take her daughter out of school.

Quite accidentally, I met Purva at a photography shop. She was sitting at the outside desk. She was able to write quite many common words in English and read and understand as well. That was enough to qualify her for this kind of job.

"Are you going to teach there next year too?" she asked me.

"You may still come to my class if you wish," I replied slowly.

"No, this place is better for me. At least now my mother doesn't ask me to wash clothes or utensils. The other girls here would be working as maid servants. Those women in our slum were asking my mother to put me into the same thing. Good that I was not completely idiot, I can read and write. That's why I got this job. I am better off than them. But I am proud of you. You are going to help so many girls and boys like me with your gift. I wish I could be there to listen to those poems. They gave me a chance."

She then gave me a card that had the name of the shop and asked me to come here if I needed photographs. Then she hugged me with her eyes closed. And at that moment, it occurred to me that she did not regret any longer but gave me a piece of her sensation of plentiful peace.

One by one, the faces had begun to disappear from the classroom and it moved me to see how the children had come to accept their destinies as inevitable. Suddenly they had made several adjustments to their life's plans. Suddenly, they had little interest in the classroom activities. They did not dislike it nor were they incapable of it but I realized that they had moved beyond it. I could sense it at times- that nibbling devouring feeling that no matter how hard they try their efforts will mean nothing, that all the words, phrases, sentences, stories and math they learnt in this one year will be crumpled in one day by the laws of the larger world. I could feel it at times what they had come to believe- that happiness and prosperity are possible only somewhere else.

They were children at heart still, but their behaviour became more like adults. Their talk changed from homework and tests to money and work. The idea that money can make things happen in the real world preoccupied them. The propellant of life was money and it was of the essence, buying them what we call a lifestyle. In their terms, it mostly meant a better house in a better slum.

By the time of the annual examination, the situation was like a ghastly dream. When I was preparing the reports for the children, I turned the pages of the registers back and forth again and again, wishing that my classroom were still as crowded as it was on my first day. It is one of my life's ironies that when I had too many students packed into a little room, I had wished that I did not have to teach in a condition like this. I could not see those children who were small in size and sat behind a taller boy. Today when the spaces in my classroom had widened, I hoped there were more arms and legs, eyes and souls to fill up those gaps. Today, my classroom looked like an empty lawn of memories that my children left behind and as I surveyed my classroom with sadness and pity, I was terrified by self-failure.

As the last unit drifted slowly, I grappled with the question of value. What did an education mean to them and what price were they willing to pay for it? Of the sixty children who had started the year with me, ten left the school. In other classrooms, the number of dropping students was extraordinarily higher. In the sixth class, twenty-three children had left the school. In the eighth class, there were twenty two pupils, fourteen of whom sought a different course by the end of the year. But these comparisons could not comfort me, for those who were quitting school spread ripples of fear among those who continued. The children did not know whose turn was next, although all of them knew that they were walking along a tightrope; that they could at any time fall into a dark inextricable abyss of non-existence. Those who would have otherwise become doctors, lawyers or engineers would soon become shopkeepers, vendors or auto-rickshaw drivers. They would fade into darkness in the way a beautiful sunset goes inside the blanket of the night. In this world where hope came very slowly, I believe my children were not sure whether to wait. One would have wished that they were dead long before they started, that their hopes never existed. Had their voyage ended? Was the path before them closed and the provisions over? Was it time 'to take shelter in a silent obscurity'?

During the time I was teaching, my children had seen the visage of a world where love and promise were abundant. I had made them believe that their lives would change forever. I had shown them how to construct a world of their own, a world that was full of wonders, a podium of values they could stand upon all their lives, an identity they could call as their own.

That world was now withering before their eyes like a burning wax candle. Now, all this was becoming a myth they could not trust. The melodies of the heart had been silenced and hope existed only in fables. How they will rage and fume to think that they have lost the bliss of heaven for the dross of the earth? No one would know what might happen to these fourteen year olds. No one knew who was to be blamed for all this. Shapeless thoughts intersected my mind.

I felt angered and broken. The poetic inspiration that I had created in my classroom had fallen like threads of silken light unwound from whirring spools. As I coped with my own failure, it seemed to me that it was meaningless to work ruthlessly hard, to bring a moment's magic to the petty lives of children. I thought I had come to offer the beauty of education but I had stirred very little to their lives other than a posy of misdirected faith. And perhaps, their hopes were shattered not by the harshness of the world they lived in but in deceit and disillusionment that a beautiful world does not really exist.

Before they left however, I had one last chance to talk to my children. It was the last class of our year and on the night before, I kept changing my lesson plan several times over. There was so much I wanted to tell before they left for life. I wanted to tell them that no matter what happened to their lives, they must never give up on their hope that a better day would come by. That they must continue to hold on to and protect their integrity and think about the choices they are taking in life and their consequences upon themselves and others. They were not limited by the experiences they have had in school or at home, but empowered by their ability to embrace self-righteousness in their daily lives.

But I did none of that. In the classroom, I stared at them with a blank expression and remembered my first day in the school. Then every day, every week and every month flashed before my eyes. I feared that if the children stared at my face long enough, they would read dejection and self-destructing pain on it. I kept holding back my aching watery eyes from yielding to the pull of gravity. Words did not come out of my mouth and my gestures that were a source of laughter for my students had stiffened.

"Can we finish the poem?" a familiar voice spoke.

As I woke up from my thoughts, I realized Dana had made the request which was met with approval from the rest of the class. I could not put down their wish. Although I had not prepared myself for a class on poetry, I riffled through the books in my bag and found a piece of paper on which I had written the poem.

The corner of my lips twitched as I started reciting the poem slowly. The words trembled out of my mouth very slowly. Gradually my throat cleared to allow my voice to reach a higher pitch. Ninety minutes had gone by without a lull. The school bell rang from downstairs to signal the end of the day but no one paid attention to it. The class had been enveloped in the immortality of the poem. Like the poet, they were unfolding a new world where they would be born again, this time with new hopes and new aspirations. One would have to carefully tread in their world for in its rich soil grew the saplings of their dreams, dreams that will live through the pavilions of time.

That day, I had explained the poem with all the pureness of the heart as if the eternal soul of the child that was living inside me had spoken itself. In the way fire kindles fire, my soul was inspired by the lives of the children in my classroom. I had lived fully each of those sixty lives.

A few weeks later, I packed my bags to return but before leaving this extraordinary place, I decided to collect some of the finest hand-crafted objects that the Peths had to offer. That day, I met Purva. The monsoon had come rushing by again. The potholes of her slum were full of rain water and frogs were resting in those holes. Seeing me from a distance, she came running in her blue-green salwar kammez holding an umbrella and splashing the water all over her salwar. It took me a while to recognize her in the rain until she got close by. She looked like a full-grown woman, suddenly.

Purva's responsibilities have increased after she left school. She was taking care of herself and the rest of her family all alone. She told me that since she had gotten to work, the boys in the neighbourhood have started to see her differently. Unable to control her excitement, she disclosed that one boy from the adjoining slum has really started to like her.

"He is a nice boy and he has studied a lot. He went to college, *like you*. And now he makes five thousand rupees already every month," she said coyly, maintaining that I was still her teacher, "But I don't think I'll marry him right away. I will stay here, work for my family until my brother gets some work and he will be able to live all by himself and help the family."

I began to see the little shacks again, the beauty parlours and saree shops around her, as the heavy smell of the morning lodged itself in my brain—I could taste the uniqueness of life in the Peth on the tip of my tongue once again. Purva hugged me and told me she'll come to visit me one day to my hometown, when she saves enough money out of her job.

Poor soul, I had thought to myself. She never stopped dreaming.

"When I have children some day, I would send them to a teacher like you," she said. "No matter what happens, I want to make sure that they can do what I could not. They will grow big one day and make you and me proud." She always rejoiced in the brightness of those little possibilities, like a fuel that she liked to burn to stay alive and kicking. I supposed that was the way she wanted to build a new world for herself.

She was still working at the shop but now she was working at two other places in shifts, as a sales girl in a sari shop and as a *mehendi* artist. By working hard and sacrificing as much as she could, she hoped to get a thousand-fold more in the life to come. She prayed that there were more hours every day for her to work. I watched her merge into the vastness of the Peth again with this confidence in her heart. And mine.

Like the poet himself, Purva roamed in thought over her universe. In her soul, I saw the spell of a living hope and the impossible struggle of the child's spirit to find a new world of wonders. With the song of poetry in her heart, she wanted to follow a star and walk toward the light in the embrace of a piercing longing for bliss. That vision was my final moment of pride.

EPILOGUE

Life is all about change, it is a process of renewal of one's self, from a seed to a flower, from flower to fruit, requiring infinite space and heaven's light to mature. If we don't change, we slow down. We stop growing. We stop journeying and submit ourselves. We repeat ourselves and no longer transform. Change happens when we face reality, when we come to understand the truth about the nature, about events and people who come into our lives. Through them, we transform ourselves into more dimensional people. This change is a movement towards becoming more fully one's own self, towards becoming complete. We learn to build greater physical and moral resources within ourselves. Just as the test of fire makes good steel, we become better people and learn to respond well to life's crude and continuing pressures.

In my own case, I believe I could have been a pawn in the endless foot-line of soldiers in India's booming software industry. I could have gone places and made a handsome lot of money. I had the degree and pedigree to do it. But I had chosen a slightly different path- a decision that can only be explained with all the tenderness of the heart. When I had come to teach in the early days of summer, I realized for the first time how widely I was alienated from these poor children by light-years of personal and cultural distances, created by the privileges of expensive private education, religion and caste. I had climbed the ladder of opportunity quite easily whereas no such ladder had ever been built for them. I knew very well that teaching children in this forgotten school will not be an easy task. In fact, the environment in the school and the neighbourhood surrounding it was so outside the ordinary that it failed every limit of the imagination which people of my background are generally endowed with. I was not really ready for this kind of a cultural adjustment.

I vividly remember the shock of the first day and the whirlwind of chaos that followed me for the next few months. I had realized that one could not become a teacher in this school by one's appointment alone. One had to strive extremely hard to earn the right to instruct such children, to educate them and lead them into the future.

Before I came here, my general life experiences had been pretty much linear; I had been loved by a mother, protected by a father, taught by great teachers, surrounded by well-to-do friends, all of which had given me my positive view of things. But this flat upbringing soon became a hurdle for me, since it left me unprepared to handle the exponentially heart-breaking realities and insensitivities of the larger world. Like most people, I never really believed that that world of tranquil certainties was about to be extinguished. I grew impatient, I got angry and frustrated every time I would walk into a slum to see half-naked children barely seven years old washing clothes, making rice or caretaking their younger siblings. The children, feral like street urchins, were so contemptuous of one another and outsiders that they could not set aside any niceties for their lives were thrown asunder the way a strong wind pulls out everything that comes in its way. At first, I did not want to believe what I was seeing. Why isn't anything done about this? What the fuck has our government been doing for so many years? I felt deeply victimised and guilty. Then I felt pathetic and powerless.

This in itself was difficult and painful for first-time teachers like me who despite being citizens of one country, had little idea about the world our children came from and who had very little capacity then to witness and survive the most impossible of human tragedies. But that did not deter me from asking questions and to continue to have a positive view of things.

But I also realized deep down that I could not hope too much for them and do too little for them. I learned to start by paying attention to what is close at hand. I learned to stand up bravely to all sorts of situations. I learned to teach in classrooms where rats attacked children every other day, and in dusty corridors, that looked more like the passageways of a juvenile prison or mental asylum; I learned to observe and argue with people who were taking reckless decisions which had turned the school into a manufactory of failure.

Those who love their country would know that it is only by striving to know a country from within that we can discover new possibilities gestating in its womb. This realization forced me to learn the ways of life of the people in the slums of Pune, their customs, their faith, their religion and their language. Before I was able to call myself a real teacher, I tried my best to put myself in their shoes so that

I could experience what it like to live in the squatters where the dignity of life had been pared down to its essence.

People live public lives in the Peth, often a tin sheet or a curtain being the only thing separating one's home from the public courtyard. So they readily formed a bond with me, whose obligations and privileges, exist only for the people who are linked by it. They made me understand what a disingenuously powerful thing it is to be able to walk in and out of people's lives easily. I realized that they did not need a roof, they did not need another spoonful of rice, all they needed was love and care. I understood, over and over again, that I need not have answers to all the questions of their lives, nor would I be able to find them, so I learned to ask them the right questions, to think of simple solutions and to assume very little.

In my earnest attempts to mingle into the credo of a society that was not mine, I had discovered that inside her heart lived millions of immured and repressed children who were in deep schism with themselves and with the rest of the world. Children did not believe me initially. For the first quarter of the year, I was the subject of their mistrust, misperception and hatred. I feared them more than they feared my own weaknesses. At that time, they were only trying to gauge when I will raise a stick to attack someone, when I will throw invectives at their castes and their parents, while I was fiercely trying to avoid a calamity in my classroom.

Slowly most of them had understood that I carried none of nefarious intent that characterized the persona of the other people in their lives. I had explained to them- and this was of primary importance- that whatever had happened to them in their lives was not their fault but the faults of cyclical maledictions that beset the places they came from. I made them believe that they needed to wake up to the consciousness in the freedom of their soul, that they were above all attacks, enmity and insults. There were days when I woke up thinking that I am going to change the way my students look at themselves. On other days, I lay awake in a cold sweat and questioned whether I could at all move the needle.

Yet, it certainly was a very difficult but fulfilling experience. It had changed in its entirety the necessities of my life and existence as also my understanding of the immense significance of education to a world so badly lacking in it. For, the children who came to Mahadeo Govind Ranade School had made me feel the distinctive dimensions of their lives and the real meaning of education for them. For, each child had a different perspective and reason for being in my class. I had unfolded its true meaning carefully.

The children in my classroom had both humbled and dignified me and the very fibre of my being was transformed by my children's optimism and sense of possibility. My experience of their world where the struggle of life is so elemental brought me into complete touch with the rest of humanity. In our struggle to understand the world and make moral calculations, we were similar. The same children, who on my first day of school bruised my eye, made me feel special and beautiful every day I entered the school. Never did they make me feel as though I was not good enough. Whenever my courage was at its lowest ebb, they had steeled me with energy. With an inexhaustible stream of hope, they taught me to get up each time after I had failed and to try again. I have learned from them how to confront the real issues of existence. They came to me with all the power, like the untamed forces of nature, and the courage to show things about myself that I did not know. In the trust they had in me, I derived all my strength. They showed me that conditions could be changed, that compassion could revive hope and that a little bit of love could do marvels. Between their shadow and their soul, I saw the luminosity of every new page where everything yet had to be written down.

My tiredness and disappointment slowly gave way to something beautiful and inspiring, the feeling of inward joy that comes to an adult from the soul of the child waking inside him. I went to school every day with a growing sense of responsibility and enthusiasm about my work. I rejoiced in discovering that the light of knowledge had lit the minds of my children and the music danced at the centre of their world. Knowledge for them was not a dead object, but rather a precious gift of life. From where I stood, I could only rejoice to see them grow, like a caterpillar which grows out of its cocoon and takes its baby steps into the gardens of life.

After my first year of teaching, six of my students had attained admissions in government and private schools, and some had won academic scholarships from the government. But I had also lost a few children from my classroom forever to the schemes of absolute failure. Yet it still contended me to think that they would walk through their lives unfettered. I knew that the children had outgrown their greatest iniquities and their divides and emerged with a stronger self and identity that was only supremely good in beneficence. To them, it was now a lie to believe that they were not worth anything. They had made peace with themselves and their surrounding world. In every moment, there was a new beginning, in every obstacle there was a new opportunity for a higher life. As a teacher and as a human being, that was my greatest achievement.

When I had joined the teaching corps, I knew I had not come here to stay forever, but to earn a life experience that I could carry with me for the rest of life, to find the eternal promise of a better and more human world. My ultimate destination was perhaps a new way of seeing things. In the course of the long aching year, I often lost faith and hope in my abilities as it constantly played hide-and-seek among society's manifold contradictions. But only hard-work and perseverance had ultimately culminated into the discovery of this promise, which was simmering beneath the surface of my endless failures. Promise that sparked through my sky like a shooting star. To the naked eye of the non-believer those sparks don't mean anything for they never undertake to lead anyone to any solid and definite conclusion, yet they glowed with an eternal welkin of light that filled my soul and lifted my heart. I had often found it in the worst of situations and pettiest of human sentiments and begun to believe in the immensity of its power. Like my children, it gave me all my aspiration for a reality that has no end to its realization- a reality that gives above all evils of life, bringing peace and purity, its cheerful renunciation of self. These beautiful things come into our lives, simply out of the blue. We may not be able to fully grasp them or understand them, but we can at least repose our trust in them. It is very easy to be defeated in the face of repeating loss and controversy, which was abundant, much harder to transcend the boundaries of self-doubt. But when one has learned how to listen to hope, then the brevity and the quickness and the childlike hastiness of one's thoughts achieve an incomparable joy. Its touch is so familiar to one's heart that it can so overwhelm one with the light of heaven that nothing can seem impossible anymore.

Through the course of my journey, I came to realize that it is only in our struggles that we can discover the hallowed greatness of life and the spiritual wisdom to strive towards humanity through meaningful work. We can stand up on our feet, garner our courage, and savour the unseen glories that truth unravels. We can put our ears to the ground and hear the laughter of little children playing on the seashore of endless worlds. We can wipe off a tear of sorrow from their eyes. We can comfort their broken souls by sharing the promise of opportunity. If we open the eyes of one little child to the light of truth and understanding, if we bring peace to the struggling and desperate mind of one teenager, we can, by showing the way, become a guiding star for some lost traveller. In return, we can find amazing powers, beyond our own, that tests us, protects us and empowers us.

AFTERWORD

My story is only a microcosm of the state of education in the country. Situations in schools and neighbourhoods elsewhere in the country are perhaps worse and while the facts and faces change, the breadth of disparity in access and quality of our education only widens. A significant proportion of our nation's children are failing in their school education at an alarmingly rate only to be disenfranchised of their most basic social, political and economic rights. This exclusion has often put in my mind a plethora of questions about this country's system of rationing out opportunities and choices for poor young children and the way education has been disrobed of its true value. Who is getting squandered and why things are the way they are? By what means would a squatter child complete school and graduate from a college? And even if he achieves the impossible, would he still get the opportunities that came my way? Would his caste, his religion and his postal address continue to raise doubts about his abilities?

During the time I taught, the government's flagship programme for universalization of education, the Sarva Shiksha Abhiyan, was entering its last phase. This programme, which I have some knowledge about through a short-lived association with the bureaucracy, has made significant strides in a country, which at the time of its independence, could not read or write. It has set up schools where there was none and encouraged nearly every child in this country to come and experience formal schooling. It has also made attempts to strengthen existing school infrastructure by providing maintenance grants in addition to school improvement grants. Two years before I began to teach, India also passed a landmark legislation, the Right To Education Act, to guarantee free, non-discriminatory and compulsory education to all its children.

Yet in spite of these novel efforts, there has been a systemic degradation of education in terms of its applicability, suitability and relevance to the educationally backward segments of this country. Several factors are perhaps responsible for this and many of them are often outside the reigns of the law and the government. But while I am no expert on education, my humble experiences made me realize that change cannot be brought about simply by enacting a law or throwing more money at the problem. Any change in the system would require a wholesale shift in the attitude of all levels of society towards education. Education must not be seen as a means to an end and therefore should not be moulded to fit the particular needs of our society or the choice of a particular culture. The principal object of education is the liberation of the human mind which can only be achieved in a world whose guiding spirit is personal love. The most important human endeavour should therefore be the striving for morality in all our deeds and actions. Our inner balance and even our very existence depend on it. Only morality in our actions can give beauty and dignity to life. And to make this a living force and bring it to clear consciousness is perhaps the foremost task of education. I learned to believe that the foundations of morality cannot be made to depend on myth nor tied to any authority lest doubt about the myth or about the legitimacy of the authority imperil the foundation of sound judgment and action.

It is possible to feel that by narrating the stories of poor children, I have only painted a patch of this country's hysterical and shameful conditions. But it is not so. The real story of a poor school is always in the custody of its poor children, their poor parents and poor teachers. It is a story that is tied in their tongue; it is verbal, protected from the rich man and his predations. Their story spoken in their own words is only as true as the purity of their hearts. Their story mattered because they carried the value of experience of things that I did not know of before, things that led me to strive to develop humility, a love for people and a genuine spirit of service of mankind. Their story has shown me that where there is faith, fear cannot exist.

I penned down my story because memories which evoked grief, shock, disappointment and loss, along with the tiny joys and victories had left open a hole in me that needed filling, a question that urgently needed answering. These memories have found a prominent place in this book because they were not the ones I had expected to witness when I first came here. I have lost myself a thousand times in these memories and although they often hurt me or took me away from myself, in the end they always led back to it. In them, I have experienced the torment of life.

Fixated with that experience, I wanted to capture the challenges and the difficulties that young boys and girls confront not only in this one school but across communities and cultures all over this country. This should not however obscure the fact that like any other school, Mahadeo Govind Ranade had hundreds of students, teachers and other people who came to school every day to accomplish and work hard at the tasks set out for them. And in the course of attaining the goals we had set out for ourselves, there were infinite smaller moments when being in the school and the neighbourhood seemed completely different, exciting and worthwhile. These memories are often lost among the stacks of bad memories but they silently keep filling the gaps that pain and confusion leave behind. Simple things bring them to mind like a prank that a child had played on me, a portrait a child had drawn of me and the endless discussions and deliberations that the teachers had amongst themselves when they prepared the children for an annual concert that had happened in the school for the first time after almost a decade. These memories still swell up like waves and then recede into the ocean of my grateful heart.

However, I am afraid that I have unfortunately managed to portray only a very small part of the whole story that took place in Mahadeo Govind Ranade School and I sincerely pray that it should be construed as a mere lack of skill rather than my sentiment. Besides the children, I had the great fortune to meet several teachers who, like me, had also come to offer the children an education and like me, they were also entangled in a string of terrific experiences. These men and women together wedged the development of my teaching abilities. From them, I have learned to observe, to follow and to act. Through their immersion, they had become potent forces in the lives of children. I do regret that I have cut short their stories. Their influence may only be perceived with the warmth of the human heart and eagerness of an open eye.

Early on I decided to write only about my students but I must at least briefly mention a few thoughts about the teachers of Mahadeo Govind Ranade School in an otherwise paltry attempt to thank them for their incredible support and camaraderie. The living and working conditions of the teachers were equally appalling to me as that of my children's. All of the teachers were struggling to survive on a miserable salary of six thousand rupees in a ridiculously expensive city. Many of them, having migrated from the very interiors of Maharashtra, lived in the pockets of various slums in flea-bitten rooms along with dozens of other people, paying as low as one hundred rupees in monthly rent. Often they did not get their salaries in time and borrowed money from one another to meet their expenses. But these teachers, despite all their differences, were still expending relentless physical and emotional efforts to make sure that a school where there was no principal and no proper administrative body continued to work in a fairly systematic way. All of us were realising that we had an important role to play.

One day, I saw Mr Awale teach his lessons in broken English, the same teacher who did not know a word of English and never supported people like me whose native language was not Marathi. He faltered and struggled to find the appropriate English words to use, but he did not give up. Later on, he had come to me and said, "I feel ashamed when children can speak and read English but a teacher like me cannot. I have decided to start teaching students in English, no matter what." I felt a bit stronger, I felt vindicated. Another teacher wanted to introduce her students to computers. She enrolled in a basic computer literacy course in the evening to get herself acquainted to computers first. She learned to type documents in Microsoft Word, use Excel, browse the internet and send emails and then taught the children the same. Our school set up its first desktop computer, although a second-hand one and badly in need of repairs, through her efforts. As the days passed, a sense of unity and brotherhood grew among most of the teachers as they slowly wanted to imitate my ways of thinking about children. Together, we began to offer value education at the beginning of every school day to combine children from Hindu and Muslim communities. Teachers came up and volunteered to teach some basic but universal human values with stories from all great religions of the country. We celebrated Rakhi, Diwali, Id, Christmas and Holi together, as an example for our children to wipe out the vices of sectarian hatred preying on their minds. Very firmly, they organised a spectacular civic campaign to help me stop people in the neighbourhood from tossing garbage onto the school compound. The very contemplation of these wonders extinguished the bitterness that I had seen in these teachers. They fuelled my ambitions and reared my faith in the capacity of every human being to transcend their condition to become someone greater than himself, to become the very models of humanity.

There was another very important person in my struggles as a teacher, the Corporator of the neighbourhood. I had visited him four times, once every month with a fresh petition to improve the school's toilet and to fill in the damaged sewers that were an immense breeding ground for water-worms and rodents, and to build in their place a closed sewage system whose contents would not empty itself behind the school compound. Every time, except the third visit, I had to meet his adjuncts. In the third visit, he had given me five minutes of his time and assured me that he would do something about it. The faintness of his assurance, at first, made me assume that it would never materialize. But sometime before the elections, the Corporator, out of his own political necessity, contributed his men and money to renovate the school's toilets, sewers and drinking water supply, while I bought fifty chairs and twenty folding tables for the children to sit during lunch. It took six months to complete all this but it paved the way for improved nutrition and sanitation outcomes in the school.

In the slums where my students lived, there were many complaints: lack of drinking water, sewage, electricity, crime, disease, broken roads and broken houses. But there was one thing that slum dwellers unanimously expected. They wanted to see a better school in its place and they were ready to pay any price for it. Because that was their ticket out of poverty. Every slum dweller knew that. Part of their vision has indeed come true as Mahadeo Govind Ranade School has seen conspicuous improvements in its facilities, faculties and spirit. Over the last four years, it has managed to avail electricity, more books for the children and is cleaner than before. Two new teachers have filled in classrooms where there was none, and an after-school center for vocational training for the girls of the school has been established. All these showed me that my journey always had a new beginning.

In the end, the very natural essence of human fellowship is fulfilled when we start believing in the worth of an individual, a worth that transcends the principles of any man-made system, when we begin to celebrate the triumph of love over hatred, dignity over doubt and unity over the unnatural divisions of mankind.